Praise for *The Madness of Grief*

'Will strike a chord with anyone who has grieved . . . shines with the sort of wry, self-analytical wisdom you might expect from Coles. Full of resonating reflections, ones that urge us all to be kinder, to love more strongly'   *Independent*

'Captures brilliantly, beautifully, bravely the comedy as well as the tragedy of bereavement . . . simultaneously heartwarming and heartbreaking, painful and strangely comforting as it confronts the reality of what happens to us all in the end'
The Times

'Bold, intimate writing . . . *The Madness of Grief* is not a manual for the bereaved, but as a vivid account of how it feels when the world suddenly falls away, it performs another kind of service'   *Sunday Times*

'Has an immediacy that is not born of long reflection and it is all the better for it'   *Financial Times*

'You don't need to be religious to find comfort in this book. Anybody who has experienced a similar complex grief will relate to many of Coles's anecdotes'   *Daily Telegraph*

'Moving and candid, this book will resonate with anyone who has lost a loved one, or has had to cope with someone they love whom they just cannot help'   *i Newspaper*

'An honest book, and a brave one'   *The Oldie*

The Reverend Richard Coles is the presenter of *Saturday Live* on BBC Radio 4. He is also the only vicar in Britain to have had a number-one hit single and appeared on *Strictly Come Dancing*. He read Theology at King's College London and after ordination worked as a curate in Lincolnshire, London and Northamptonshire. He is the author of many works of non-fiction as well as the Canon Clement mystery series – the first of which, *Murder Before Evensong*, was an instant *Sunday Times* no.1 bestseller.

THE MADNESS OF GRIEF

A MEMOIR OF LOVE AND LOSS

The Reverend Richard Coles

WEIDENFELD & NICOLSON

First published in Great Britain in 2021 by Weidenfeld & Nicolson
This paperback edition published in 2022 by Weidenfeld & Nicolson
an imprint of The Orion Publishing Group Ltd
Carmelite House, 50 Victoria Embankment
London EC4Y 0DZ

An Hachette UK Company

1 3 5 7 9 10 8 6 4 2

ISBN (Mass Market Paperback) 978 1 4746 1963 9
ISBN (eBook) 978 1 4746 1964 6
ISBN (Audio) 978 1 4746 1965 3

Typeset by Input Data Services Ltd, Somerset

Printed and bound in Great Britain by Clays Ltd, Elcograf S.p.A.

www.weidenfeldandnicolson.co.uk
www.orionbooks.co.uk

IM
David Coles
Priest

Psalm 132 vi

Contents

Preface

It is now two and half years since my husband David Coles died, and a year since the publication of *The Madness of Grief* in hardback.

'It does exactly what it says on the tin,' a friend said, who had patiently and generously put up with the mess of the just-bereaved me in the first days and weeks of my widower-hood, when she read the book in proof.

We were talking the other day. 'Do you think I am mad now?' I asked her. 'No,' she replied, 'but you're different.' She asked me what it was like to read now what I had written then.

In truth, I cannot really remember writing it. Partly because of the unreality of everything we did in lockdown viewed from a world returned more or less to normal, but also because I have had two and a half years of a very different existence – one without the material David.

At first, he was surprisingly present; seen in a glimpse, res-urrected by a faint puff of aftershave released from a pillow or by the dogs still primed to the timetable of his daily existence. A lot of the effort of the book went into curating those frag-ments of his continuing existence, hoarding them against the raids of time and forgetfulness. That slowly began to change as I began to understand that we must let go.

One of my favourite paintings is Titian's *Noli me Tangere* in the National Gallery. It shows the scene from John's gospel, when Mary Magdalene goes to Jesus's tomb on Easter Morning and finds it empty. Weeping, she is disturbed by a gardener – Titian shows him holding a hoe – but when she asks him where they have taken him, he replies with her name, and she realises who he really is: Jesus, risen from the grave.

She falls to her knees and reaches out to him, but he recoils, saying *Noli me tangere*, do not touch me. So real, so human, so affecting, like Titian you can imagine it happening in front of you. Except it didn't, or not like that. *Noli me tangere* – do not touch me – is taken from the Latin translation of the Bible made by St Jerome, the version the painters of the Renaissance would have known. But in the original Greek the verb *haptou* has continuous force, so it is not so much *do not touch me*, but rather *do not cling to me*. Jesus is not saying, I am now beyond you, you cannot approach me, I am untouchable – he's saying I cannot stay, I have somewhere to be, things to do, let me go.

I have just retired as Vicar of Finedon, and moved away from the house David and I shared in the parish we loved, to start a new life. My last visit before I left was to my beloved's grave, in the churchyard of a little village near Finedon where we had a cottage. His grave was marked by a temporary wooden cross because lockdown delayed the delivery of the headstone I had made for him. Finally it arrived, and was installed with me and his mum and dad looking on. It was an even more significant moment than I expected, a permanent monument to him at last, and a marker for me too. I felt let go.

An ending, a new beginning, but nothing ever really ends. Carved into his headstone is a quotation from Psalm 65, thy clouds drop fatness, they shall drop upon the dwellings of the wilderness: and the little hills shall rejoice on every side

The fastidious observer will note that there is no full stop after 'every side'. This is not an oversight on the part of the letterer but a deliberate anticipation of the arrival of my own headstone when I die and go in next to him, which continues the quote:

the folds shall be full of sheep: the valleys also shall stand so thick with corn, that they shall laugh and sing.

If you have been bereaved and go weeping to a grave I hope you too will one day laugh and sing again.

May 2022

There was a ring on the vicarage doorbell one day, and when I answered it, I found a woman standing there. She was ripe in years, barefoot and holding a half-empty bottle of brandy – neither being unusual for her. What was unusual was that she was wearing a wedding dress. Behind me our five dachshunds began to bark.

'Father Richard?' she said.

'Yes?'

'Will you marry me?'

'To whom, Pauline?'

'You.'

'You want to marry me?'

'I do . . . I do, I do, I do, I do, I do,' she sang, like ABBA.

'Afraid I can't do that.'

She looked at me with suspicion. 'Why not?'

'Because Father David got there first. You know this.'

She tilted her head to one side and thought about it. Then she said, 'So you won't marry me?'

'No, I'm afraid not.'

She lowered her head and went into a sort of boxer's stance. 'Then I'm going to blow you to fucking kingdom come.'

'How will you do that, Pauline?'

'With a BOMB!'

I

'Do you have a bomb? I can't see one.'

'I AM A FUCKING BOMB!'

'Well, please don't explode,' I said, and wondered if what she had said qualified as a threat with a weapon, in which case if I called it in the police would have to send a van, a costly procedure which had happened before. On the other hand, if it kept on happening, police involvement would make a mental health assessment more likely and improve her chances of receiving inpatient care, which we had been trying to sort out for some time.

'I've already exploded,' she said. 'I AM THE EXPLOSION.'

I remembered this as I walked around Kettering on a cold December day. Father David, who 'got there first', had died. I had enough of my wits about me to know where I was, to recognise the shops and the pubs and the petrol stations, and I had my phone, and my debit card, everything I needed to buy the necessities of life: milk, bread, *Private Eye*, dog food.

This time I am the explosion. I have just detonated, but in such super slow motion, you would not notice at first that I am disintegrating in front of you, micrometre by micrometre, in the madness of grief.

Friday the Thirteenth

Friday, 13 December 2019, ill-starred day, began with Boris Johnson walking into Number Ten as Prime Minister for the first time since his re-election. It ended for me in ICU at Kettering General Hospital.

The day before I had given a speech at the annual luncheon for suppliers to the dental profession in London. I always enjoy these things, being nosy, and because they pay me, but I particularly enjoyed this because I sat next to a man who told me a story that left me very moved. He was in his late forties, prosperous, fit, the kind of man who can reverse-park a caravan using only mirrors and with one hand on the wheel. We fell into conversation over smoked salmon, and he said how much he had wanted to hear me speak, not least because last year his teenaged son came out as gay to him and his wife.

'Did you see it coming?' I asked. 'No, not at all.' 'Was that difficult?' 'No. I was just glad he chose to tell us before he told anyone else.' 'How's he doing?' 'Fine. I offered to go with him to tell his grandparents and uncles and cousins, but he said no, he'd rather do it on his own. And he did. I was so proud of him.'

He had to collect himself for a second. 'I met my wife', he said, 'thirty years ago on holiday in Portugal. We were

3

seventeen. It was love at first sight. I love her more than anyone, apart from my children. You know what we danced to? The Communards. Thank you for the music.' Solid handshake again.

When I got back to the vicarage David and I shared in the parish of Finedon, Northamptonshire – where I am the vicar and he, to his irritation, a de facto vicar's spouse, although ordained himself – I wanted to tell him about this encounter. But he was in his dressing gown and lying in front of the fire with the dogs, a pile of bloodstained tissues, like scattered carnations, encircling him.

'Hospital, now,' I said.

He said no. I said, 'You've got to go to hospital' – this had happened many times before – and he said no. I said, 'Phone the doctor,' and he said he had, and the doctor had told him to go to hospital. 'SO GO TO HOSPITAL,' I said. He refused. Why?

'Because they'll admit me, and I will lie on a trolley all night waiting for a specialist to see me in the morning. I might as well sleep in my own bed and go first thing. You have to pick up my admission papers from the surgery when it opens at twenty past eight. And a prescription. And you'll need to get the meds – not from Burton, ours.'

This was form we had followed before, and David was expert in it, not only from being an experienced patient, but from years of experience as a nurse in A&E before he was ordained.

The next day I got up, but he was not to be seen. He quite often slept out in the summer house when he was unwell, so he wouldn't wake me if he was up in the night. He had built the summer house for me as a fiftieth birthday present, and it is lovely, very *Homes and Gardens*, piled high with cushions and pillows, fitted with a sound system and a wood burner that produced a thready plume of smoke through the chimney, so I knew he was At Home.

I did not want to wake him, so I went straight to the surgery, arriving just as it opened. The receptionist was waiting at the door with an envelope. She handed it to me with the look of sympathetic urgency spouses of difficult patients get to recognise. I should have thought more about that, perhaps, but I was used to it, and there was nothing particularly unusual about my day so far. My next stop was the pharmacy in the village, but it had not yet opened, so I went to the cafe, rewarding myself for this delay with a bacon butty and a cappuccino and a flick through social media.

When the pharmacy opened, I picked up David's prescription and headed home. He still wasn't up, so I went to the summer house where I found him in his clothes sitting on the sofa, holding an ice bucket half-filled with what I thought was something from the pottery he had built in the garage, a dark brown granular liquid, some sort of slip. And then he vomited into it and I saw it was coming from inside him. And then I saw that the cushions and the rug were stained with it too.

'Ambulance, now,' I said. And he, with unusual meekness, nodded.

I dialled 999, and felt the first surge of alarm when the voice that replied asked the pro forma questions – just get here, I thought, but didn't say. Within ten minutes a car pulled up and a paramedic got out, impeccably made-up, which I thought strikingly glamorous for her dark green uniform, half paramilitary, half garden-centre. The dogs began to bark at this intruder, so I shut them in my study, and showed her the way to the summer house. Over the door is a sign in slate saying *Wahnfried* – my idea, named after Wagner's villa at Bayreuth. It means Free from Care, and never did it seem more unsuitably named, for she looked worried, and got straight to work, and called for an ambulance. I said the first of many stupid things I said that day:

'Was I right to dial 999?'

She looked at me for a second before replying, 'Yes.'

I smarted, in the way we do when professionals are at work in our houses, when your space is for that moment their space, and they show insufficient regard for your vase, or your social entitlement as host. I thought lots of incon-sequential and irrational things about getting the 10.05 from Wellingborough to get to work at the BBC, and about having to rearrange things so I could get to Bishopsgate in the City in the evening to preside at my first carol service for the Leathersellers' Company, having just been made their honorary chaplain.

An ambulance arrived. David was by now cannulated and not quite making sense, and they put him in a chair because, I guessed, vomiting made it impossible for him to lie flat. As the dogs went bananas behind my study door, they wheeled him through the vicarage to where the ambulance was wait-ing on the drive, and he crossly shouted at me the things he would need for his overnight bag. The list was long and pre-cise. In the past, when this had happened, I invariably failed to pack the right dressing gown, or chose a day rather than a night moisturiser, or put in his knitting when he wanted his sewing. As this was going on, domestic nonsense in contrast to the medics' urgency, my neighbours' daughter went by walking the dog and, tactfully, pretended not to notice as a bloody David was wheeled past, while I, in vicar mode, wished her good morning, as if nothing were unusual. And then they drove him away to the general hospital.

I went back inside, sat down and had a cup of coffee, and then went upstairs to curate the overnight bag he would need for this stay, which would involve a blood transfusion, I supposed, like last time. So it could be a day or two, in which case every conceivable option would need to be provided (David had once insisted I bring to hospital his Celtic harp). I did this without great urgency, because, on past experience, it would take time for him to be triaged, treated, admitted, and emerge on the other side in the ward, when this bag would be required. Even so, I find it quite extraordinary now that the sight of my beloved vomiting blood as he was stowed in an ambulance did not particularly alarm me. Maybe the brain offers consciousness manageable scenarios?

I checked the bag again, and then again for Marlboro Lights and Zopiclone, his diurnal and nocturnal essentials, let the dogs out for a pee, and made some phone calls to rearrange my day. Then I drove to the hospital, with his bag in the boot alongside mine, with the kit I would need – cassock, surplice, scarf and hood – for the carol service later. Clergy used to get free parking at hospitals – that seems as wildly generous now as school milk or pensioner TV licences – but no longer, and, regardless of circumstances, like medics we too must pay for our parking, assuming we can find a space. When there are no spaces, I normally park at the crematorium just up the road, where we are still considered on the team, and parking is more freely available. But I was under pressure, so used the expensive short-stay hospital car park, because the cheaper double-decker was full.

I wouldn't be long. Once he was on the ward I could leave for London and, instead of staying over, come home after the carol service to take care of the dogs, then in the morning take the early train to London to be in Broadcasting House for *Saturday Live*. By then I would have a clearer idea about how long he would be in hospital. Anyone who has looked after someone with a chronic medical condition will know what this is like, rearranging the schedule, and dog care, and what you need to take with you and where and when, mobilising friends with visiting rights, as you try to live a functional life around the dysfunction the condition causes. I had got quite skilled at it, of necessity, having responsibilities in the parish which take up, theoretically, half my time, and in the other half earning a living in the media, being what David liked to call a 'borderline national trinket'.

A&E was all but full, as usual, and I thought it would be a long wait on a hard chair but when I reported at reception they said someone would take me to a waiting room. I followed a nurse past the benches of the halt and the lame and the aged and the asthmatic and saw among them the Lord Lieutenant of Northamptonshire, not in his ceremonial uniform but holding one of those grey cardboard bowls. 'Hello,' he said. 'Hi,' I said, and then we both looked away, knowing only the briefest of pleasantries was proper in these circumstances.

It was not a waiting room but a staff room, with a kettle and nurses' biscuits, and a keypad lock on the door. Nurses coming in would look slightly surprised to see me there; one wondered what I was doing, and asked me to make sure the door was kept shut. How precious, I thought, is your own invaded space in an A&E full of the sick and frightened and frustrated. Another had lost her keys, and we all got on our hands and knees looking for them (unsuccessfully). And then after about an hour another 'Hello!' It was a couple who had taken one of our dachshund puppies, Roger the Sausage. They had come in with the wife's father, and were waiting for him to be assessed. We talked about the dogs, about the characteristics of dachshunds, and then a medic in scrubs came in and said they needed me. 'See you in a bit,' I said, and followed her into a treatment area and through parted plastic curtains.

David was lying on his side on a trolley, vomiting blood copiously. Around him stood three or four medics in scrubs. One of them held out to me a piece of paper, stained with blood. It was a consent form. I glanced at it, and it said something about options, and risks, and something about a risk of death, and I said, 'Ooh, let's not do the one with a risk of death, please,' and looked for a reaction to my campery, but they just looked at me.

David said, 'He doesn't understand, give us a minute.'

The medics left. David pulled me towards him until my forehead rested on his. It felt warm and clammy. And, very matter of fact, he said, 'They are going to operate, but I might die. I love you.'

I started to say 'I love you too' but my voice broke, and then the medics were suddenly back in the bay, surrounding us, and said they had to get him to theatre immediately and they wheeled him away and I signed the consent form and my hands began to shake. A nurse said he would take me somewhere in ICU where I could wait, and I went to collect David's bag from the waiting room, now empty.

'Are you OK?' the nurse asked.

'This is . . . devastating . . .' was all I could say. He took me out through the back of A&E and on to the main corridor. We passed Costa on the way and I heard a voice say, 'Oh look, it's the *Strictly* Rev! Do us a twirl, Rev!'

I pretended not to hear, but then a couple came over and said, 'Can we have a selfie? My mum . . .' (always the mum, I thought) '. . . LOVES you!'

And so as David was being prepped for surgery I stood outside Costa doing selfies for people – smile, thumbs up – and later wondered if they would see in their pictures that

I had congealed blood on my hands and was white with shock.

My first engagement since David's death: I am giving a series of talks on a cruise liner, an annual event scheduled for January because David hates the winter and it gets us to the Caribbean, where we have a week on a beach while England is at its grimmest. We have ten days on board first, which David adores, not least because the company accommodates us generously and he loves to throw parties on our balcony when the weather turns from mid-Atlantic winter to Caribbean sun.

But I am travelling alone now; not only a turn, and therefore recognisable to people on board, but recognisable as a widow after the media coverage of David's death, one of the dozens and dozens of widows who take to cruising in search of company, to meet someone new, or just to get away from the weather. They know my fate and are sympathetic, happy to talk and share tips, but I feel very alone without him, a table for one, no hope of a debrief about other passengers, or what he's learned in his craft class, or who we are going line dancing with next. So I pick a shorter route, embarking on an inbound ship from the Azores, which I choose because I have never been there before. But my luggage does not arrive from Lisbon and I have a day before we embark for Southampton walking its cobbled streets of black-and-white houses in stubble and a day-old shirt. David would have hated that.

I love being at sea, a discovery of middle age, and the loneliness of fresh widowhood is palliated by the pleasure of being alone on deck looking towards the horizon, when the restless ripple and froth of the sea's surface resolves into a dark steely blue.

I remember being alone on deck on a ship in the North Atlantic, between St Kilda and Iceland, midsummer, nearly midnight, but still light, the sea calm and greenish, and nothing to see in any direction, and two kilometres of depth beneath us. I was not alone, as it happened. A woman was also looking at the horizon and she came alongside me at the rail, and we fell into conversation, as people do when their attention is fixed on something else. She was in her late eighties and had lived an extraordinary life, which she told me in a matter-of-fact and un-self-regarding way.

'What would you like to do with your life now?' I asked.

'I only want one thing,' she said. 'A noble death.'

'What would that be like?'

'I don't know. I wouldn't mind going down on this ship.'

I don't really remember much between then and arriving at ICU. We must have taken the stairs up a floor, or got in a lift, but in my memory's itinerary it was one gliding movement along one plane. I've no idea why.

I made small talk with the nurse, who was kind, but not in shock like me, and I don't know if what I said connected with what he said as he put me into the waiting room. ICU is in the new wing, not long opened, and smarter than the rest of the hospital. Soft colours, IKEA furnishings, like a youth court or done-up dole office. Intended to soothe, I suppose, but that has the opposite effect I find when brute reality is your reason for being there.

I sat on a chair at a low table, looking at a vending machine and wondering what to do. There was a family waiting there too, who said hello. I think they were Travellers from their accents, and from their ease with a man in a dog collar, and from the swelling of their ranks, as more and more family arrived.

What should I do? I texted my editor at *Saturday Live*, who understood immediately and said not to worry, she would sort out a last-minute stand-in for the programme. I decided to phone family too, so I called my older brother and his wife, and said, 'I'm in ICU in Kettering General. David's been admitted and it's not looking good.'

'What can we do?'

'Nothing, I think. I just wanted to let you know.'

'Oh, OK.'

'Bye then.'

'Bye.'

One of the women from the family also waiting there came and said hello. She was about my age. Her grandson had been admitted with breathing difficulties, he had a condition that made him susceptible. She asked me to pray for him, and I said I would, of course, and for her and her family, but she must have worked out that I was not there on duty, because she asked me why I was there.

'My partner,' I said, 'they're operating on him now.'

If I had not been in shock, I don't know if I would have volunteered this information, because Travellers, it is often said, are not gay-friendly, and a priest with another man for a partner might be even further beyond the pale. But she was completely unfazed by it and was just kind and said that she would pray for me.

My phone went. It was my brother. 'Do you want us to come?'

'Yes, I think I do.'

'We're on our way.'

I looked at the phone in my hand and saw that it was already lunchtime and that I had to tell people what was happening.

The next call was, I thought, an easy one. I called the Leathersellers' Company, and asked to speak to the events coordinator. I told her where I was and that I would not be able to make it to the carol service, but my voice went and I couldn't speak, and she, tenderly, filled in the informational gaps, and told me she would sort it out.

Then I called David's mum in Lancashire. 'Hello, Richard?' she said, already a note of anxiety sounding at this unexpected call. I normally stay in touch with the in-laws via Messenger, only David's medical mishaps meriting a call.

'David's in hospital, Irene, he's in theatre. It's not looking great, you need to come down.'

I gave her directions, told her where to find us in the hospital. She and Vinnie, my father-in-law, would be there as soon as possible, three hours from Chorley to Kettering, after they'd got someone to look after the dog.

The dog. Our dogs. We had five and they were on their own at home. I called our friend Sarah, who has a key, and told her what was happening, and she said she would take care of them. And then I sat and talked to the family of the boy with breathing difficulties about nothing in particular, making sure I had a view of the door, which sometimes buzzed and admitted visitors. I was hoping it would admit my brother Andy and his wife Louise, but it next opened to admit a clutch of grave-looking medics in their playroom-style scrubs, and they looked at me, and before one came towards me, I was up and heading for the half-opened door to the relatives' room.

We sat down on comfy chairs, and I saw on the coffee table a box of tissues, one helpfully teased out in the direction of the chair I was offered, intimating its tragic purpose.

An older doctor – the surgeon? – said medical things as a preamble, and I nodded along as if I understood what he was talking about. When I had visited parishioners in intensive care I would sometimes stand beside their beds looking thoughtfully at the screens, as lively with data as video games, as if I were interpreting them.

'. . . cannot control the bleed . . . blood pressure too low . . . unable to operate . . . very small chance of survival . . .'

After a few seconds of this, I worked out that he was not dead. 'What's the situation now?'

'We can't do anything more for him. We could risk an operation, but it would mean going to Leicester, and he would almost certainly not survive the journey.'

I could see that he was a solved medical problem as far as they were concerned, but I had other matters in mind. I needed to know if he was going to die.

'This is . . . devastating . . .' I said again, and they nodded sympathetically. 'What's your best medical advice on how to proceed?' I must have sounded like Captain Mainwaring,

'Make him comfortable, and put him on end-of-life care.'

End-of-life care. He is going to die. I felt an impulse surge to heroically save him, I wanted the junior doctor to raise her hand and say, 'There's a thing I once saw at medical school . . .,' to demand an air transfer, for a medical team to be flown in from Cedars Sinai, where David had worked in the ER years ago, so they would do it for nothing.

That impulse ebbed. I knew he was going to die. 'What happens?'

'We'll admit him to ICU, make him comfortable, and when the time is right, withdraw ventilation and let him slip away.' I thought of a song I wrote with Jimmy Somerville in the eighties called 'Don't Slip Away'.

'OK,' I said. 'His parents are coming down from Chorley. It might be a couple of hours.'

'When you're ready.'

They got up and went, apart from a junior doctor who asked, kindly, if I was OK. I said I wasn't, but my brother was coming. She left and I sat in the relatives' room for a few minutes, not sure whether what had just happened had really happened. Not sure what I should do next. I kept thinking of our song.

Now that I've got you in my arms
won't let you slip away,
now that I've got you in my arms
won't let you slip a-waaaay.

I went back to the waiting area.

'Are you all right, Father?'

'No, I'm not. He's not going to make it.'

As soon as I said it, I saw I had to make a decision. Should I phone Irene, by now somewhere on the M6, and tell her he was not going to survive? What good would it do? It would only make her more anxious than she already was. But others needed to know, his brothers and sister, and family, and I did not have all their numbers.

Then my brother and his wife arrived. It was not the first time I had scrambled him when David was in trouble, perhaps because he is my older brother, and that's my default, or because as a former cop he is not easily fazed. I wanted people around who would not be fazed. There is something self-contained and steady about Andy, an unflinching quality which was perhaps acquired through thirty years' service in the Met, or maybe was always there? I have a photograph of him dressed as a cowboy when he was about six, and he looked as steady on his hobby horse then as he does on his trail bike, folly of retirement, today. He has also started to look like my father: high forehead, balding and, characteristic of the men of our family, rather lacking in sartorial *sprezzatura*. In contrast, Louise was full of *sprezzatura*, beautiful, intelligent, outgoing and kind. She and David had immediately got on, sharing a wildness and spontaneity that Andy and I do not share. She and David used to go off on unauthorised expeditions, to France – she was a French teacher, and David used to live there – and to North Africa, which they both loved, and Louise knew well, having lived for ten years in Cairo. David loved it too, not least for the opportunities for wildly extravagant purchasing in souks. He would time his arrival home from these trips when I was out, and by the time I got back the dining room or the summer house had been transformed into a harem or a bazaar.

I told them what had happened, and that David was not going to survive, the telling of facts at war with the chaos I was feeling, and I do not know if I made any sense. Just then a porter wheeled a bed past us and I looked and saw that it was David, unconscious and on a ventilator, but I had important information to impart and while my eyes followed him, my mouth kept talking about his condition, preferring to deal with the information rather than with seeing him for the first time since the bay in A&E, when he was fully conscious and able to speak to me, and now he was unconscious and I did not know if I would be able to speak to him again.

'. . . a gastro-intestinal bleed which they are not able to repair because his blood pressure is too low and if they tried to transfer him to Leicester he would not survive the transfer . . .'

And I saw that Andy and Louise were not listening to me but looking at David, paused outside the second set of double doors which led to the ward and the rooms where patients were treated. One of the medics was looking for a key card to open the doors, but I wanted the doors not to open, for the process of his end-of-life care to halt, because a mistake had been made, a judgement reached too hastily, human error, and the state-of-the-art machinery of the spanking new ICU ward would not admit him to the place where he was due to spend his last hours. Don't open, don't open, I thought, but they opened and he went through and I ran out of things to explain.

I suddenly remembered I was due to meet two friends for lunch in London. I had been particularly looking forward to it because they knew each other only by repute, and wanted to know each other for real. I was the means by which that was finally going to happen – a role I enjoy for it feeds the need to be the agent of good things. I texted Linda to say I couldn't come because David was ill. She texted back to say they would meet anyway, which I was glad about, and asked how David was, so I said he was dying. There it was, written down, and I hesitated to send it, partly because my first feeling was not to let anyone know who did not need to know. I had every confidence in my friend's discretion, which is why I did press send, but my instinct was to go off grid. I did not want anyone in the media to get wind of it and have to deal, or find someone to deal, with enquiries. And – more than that – sending that word 'dying' out into the world beyond the circle around David gave it a reality which I wanted to deny, or at least control.

Death is the enemy, and we want to contend, so we try to establish rules of engagement for a fair fight, but there is no fair fight, and there are no rules of engagement. You have no power.

We went to sit down in our corner of the waiting room, a corner by now under pressure as more family members for the boy with respiratory problems arrived. We formed a corral of chairs in our corner, trying to keep some space to ourselves and what was happening to us, and I knew there would soon be more coming and we would need chairs for them too. My brother, always practical, asked if there was anyone he could call. Yes, Will, my younger brother, and while he did that I called my PA so she could get on with cancelling appointments for the following day. 'The day, darling Richard?' she said. 'Let me clear your diary.'

Yes, of course. I felt, for the first time, the intricate apparatus of my organised life stall, and realised that none of that was important now. I felt too the wasp-buzz of anxiety about missing appointments, disappointing people, losing revenue, fade to be replaced by something new: the arrival of dread, like an ice shelf gliding in from the Antarctic.

'You can come and see him now,' said a nurse. And we went through another set of doors, slathering ourselves dutifully with hand sanitiser first, and into one of the rooms.

I knew the room. A parishioner of mine had fought a long and eventually victorious battle for his life in it, and I had spent hours there with his family as the medics got his condition under control. The beds, which look like something from *Alien*, face the door not the window and seem marooned in the middle of the room, which David would have hated. Whenever we arrived at a rented cottage on holiday he would send me to the supermarket while he rearranged the furniture and got the cushions right, so the design elements and light volumes would 'flow' properly. This space, lit with work light rather than domestic light, was arranged so medics could get to him and to the machinery, which bleeped and winked and displayed his vital signs.

And there on the bed he lay, calm and still, intubated and cannulated. To me this was a relief. The last time I had seen him was in chaos and blood, but I saw shock in the faces of my brother and sister-in-law, seeing how wasted he looked.

In dramas on film and television the occupants of

deathbeds are serene and composed, albeit not looking their best. In reality no one looks good in ICU; the breathing tube tugging at the side of the mouth so it looks like a grimace, and the battery of devices putting things in and taking things out, making them look so vulnerable, so dependent on tubes and plugs and constant attention from the nurses, who were gentle with him and gentle with us.

Can he hear me? Is he in any pain? What will happen?

They said to talk to him as I normally would, and I did, singing our private repertoire of songs in his ear, unembarrassed to do so in front of Andy and Louise and the nurses. I wanted him to know I was there, and I thought the nonsense rhyme to the tune of the 'Jolly Farmer' by Schumann might get through to parts of him that could still engage with the external world. I don't know if it did, for he was deeply sedated, beyond pain, so the machine could breathe for him.

What will happen?

'When the time is right, we will take out his breathing tube, and let nature take its course. He might just fade and go very quickly, but he might not. Whatever happens, we'll take good care of him.'

Louise and Andy went to get coffee from the Costa downstairs, and I went out to the corridor to call Irene.

'Richard?' I could hear the dread in her voice and the sound of traffic and lorries rumbling in the background.

'Irene, I'm really sorry, but he's not going to make it . . .' I could not say any more. She made an anguished sound. After a moment I said, 'I'm sorry to tell you like this, but I thought you would want to let the family know.'

I could hear her speaking to Vinnie, indistinctly, and then she came back on the phone. She had already told his brothers and sister. Mark was on his way from Lancashire and Andrew would be coming from Northampton. His sister,

Mandy, was about to go into hospital and couldn't come. 'Hang on, David, hang on, David,' Irene said.

'He's on a ventilator and they'll keep him on it until everyone's here.'

As I ended the call it struck me that I had just said the worst thing to Irene and Vinnie that anyone could say. And that they were now sitting in a little metal box on the M6, in Friday traffic, full of dread and anticipation, with a hundred miles to go.

The dead person persists most durably at the edge of things, in the unconscious habits which have accommodated them, impervious to the fact of their death. I sometimes think this is what ghosts are, flickers across the edge of sense anticipating the presence of the absent one. The first time it happened to me I was in the sitting room and looked to my left. I had draped a throw he liked to wear when he was cold over the post at the bottom of the banisters, and it hung there, rather like it did on him when he was bony and pale. My eye read it as him, and I saw him, with my mind's eye, standing on the bottom step at the beginning of his laborious ascent. I say my mind's eye, it was as real as reality and my heart skipped before my mind reasserted the knowledge of his death. I remember my father, not given at all to flights of supernatural fancy, saw both his parents after their death in this way, his father in the garden, his mother at her desk.

David haunts me too, even now, by olfactory means. I sometimes smell cigarette smoke, usually at the bottom of the stairs, which used to enrage me when he was living. It is a jarring feeling to be both annoyed that he has broken the rules and relieved that he is still present in these spectral fumes.

My younger brother Will and his wife, Julia, arrived. Will and I have a strong resemblance – he is a bit taller, and, on a good day for me, a bit heavier – so strong when I look at him I think I see myself as others see me. I saw in his face distress which gave me a measurement for my own. Julia is head of a school for children with special needs and Will has worked in social care for children and young people all his career, so like Andy they are used to crises. But this was David and me in crisis, and I think a part of me was alarmed by seeing not professional detachment in them but distress.

The medics did not show distress. David was their patient, not their brother-in-law or friend or partner, and I wanted to see detachment because it felt like it could serve as a shield for me, some protection against the catastrophe which I did not want to accept, and could not believe.

I have been at many deathbeds. Some of them in a professional role, but several personal, and intimate, thirty years ago. For a gay man living in a big city like London in the eighties and nineties, deathbeds came frequently as HIV rampaged its way through our circle of friends and intimates. When the first of my friends died, in 1986, I was twenty-four and immortal, as we all were. I heard of his death minutes before I went on stage to perform 'Don't Leave Me This Way' in a TV studio in Barcelona. The record was number one there, and we were top billing, so we were obliged to grin at the audience and cameras and mime a song which expressed the futile wish for someone to stay. How apt, because, to paraphrase Damien Hirst, the thought of death is impossible in the mind of the living – or it was then.

That changes once the possibility of death suddenly lands like a dropped anvil. When you have experienced that, there is no going back, no prelapsarian state, innocent of mortality, where you may live again. The memory fades, the wound heals – or so you think. I don't think it does fade, really; you just don't look in that direction, until you walk through a door and find it there, unchanged, waiting for you.

Irene and Vinnie came in through the door. Irene almost ran to David's bed and took his hand. Vinnie, grey-faced, observed the elementary pleasantries with me, the necessary formalities of company, but they fell away, like rain off hostas, as he looked at his youngest son on his deathbed. Irene said that she thought this would happen one day, and I wondered if that helped or not, now that day had arrived.

As they sat at his bedside, I saw him in them: the shape of his mother's face, his father's dark eyes and hair, Armada Irish, David thought, with heritage in that country. David had reinvented himself so often, made himself over so often, that his past was not always obvious to see in his present, but I did see it in his parents, not only the physical characteristics but personality too: Irene's energy and Vinnie's doggedness.

It was not so obvious now. David was so pale he was almost the colour of chalk, paler for his dark hair, touches of silver now, and his dark eyes, which made me think of a figure from Munch. But he was very thin, and his head looked too big for his neck and shoulders, and he was so delicate, sustained only by the machinery that was getting oxygen into his lungs and into his body.

I remembered once coming to paediatric ICU in the same hospital with David to baptise the newborn, very premature, son of a parishioner, and seeing the delicacy with which David warmed the baptismal water to body temperature and squeezed a droplet onto the baby's little head – 'I baptise you in the name of the Father, and of the Son, and of the Holy Spirit' – while we prayed that he would live. He did, and thrived, and I now see him kicking a football round the Rec, unaware of the desperate prayers we had said in the soft light of the incubator. I looked at David's hand in his mother's and remembered the baby's mother reaching into the incubator and placing her wrist under her son's tiny feet so, she said, her pulse would transmit strength to his. I could see the pulse in Irene's wrist and prayed, hopelessly, that hers would strengthen his.

After a while, when they had spent some time with him, and held his hand and kissed him and told him they were there, I suggested we go for a cup of tea in the family room. Irene and Vinnie, true Lancastrians, rank tea just a little below air in the hierarchy of needs.

There were practical matters to deal with. I did not know how long they would want to stay – one night, two nights, a week? – but I could not put them up at the vicarage for now. There was too much evidence of the night before, and too much of David's precipitous decline, and I could not bear the thought of them seeing it. I offered to put them up in the hotel next to the hospital, but they would not hear of me paying for it. I insisted, in the slightly aggressive British way of hospitality, and, I suppose, to try to exercise some power over circumstances. We reached an impasse. 'Let's worry about it later,' said Irene. 'What's going to happen?' said Vinnie.

I explained what had been explained to me and when I said 'and let him fade away . . .' I felt again a stab of betrayal that I was colluding in the medical abandonment of a forty-three-year-old man only halfway through an extraordinary life. I wondered if Irene would be angry with me and shout 'DO SOMETHING!' She didn't. We all knew how ill he was, and how ill he had been before, and that he would not make old bones. One thing to know that, another to be summoned to his deathbed.

Did I sound detached, uncaring, unmoved? I could only deal consciously with a fraction of what was happening, the parts I could cope with – accommodation, dog care, tea – because David's death was unthinkable even though it was happening right in front of us. I have seen this at many a deathbed, and I have also seen it cause terrible friction between those attending, because what we are able to deal with may not be the same. I have seen people on the edge of physical violence when one daughter wanted a nurse to give vitamins to her dying father, which her sister thought insultingly insensitive.

I had none of that with Vinnie and Irene. There was no disagreement, and if they felt any, they made a brilliant job of keeping it to themselves. I could not have asked for more from the in-laws, from them, and from David's brother Mark, who was the next to come through the door. Mark and David look quite alike, though Mark is thinner, wirier, and has one of those lacy tattoos that covers his forearm – not that he would think of it as lacy. Like David he is dressy, a hat wearer, rather a dandy, but there is a toughness about him, a degree of self-possession which David could not always match – big brother little brother dynamic – and sometimes I would see David in Mark and sometimes not. He had driven down from Lancashire too, where he lives not far from his parents with his wife and two sons. He and David had always been closest, in age and affinity, although David had been distant in illness, not wanting anyone to know about it, especially when his appearance could not be ignored. He was adamant about this, so I'd sometimes had off-the-record conversations with Irene to reassure her, but I could not reassure anyone now, and Mark's face, when he came into the room, looked to me like another monitor of vital signs, displaying in vivid metrics David's decline. 'Our kid,' he said, sotto voce, as he sat next to David, temporarily in deathbed pole position.

Mark gave up that position to Andrew, their oldest brother, whose Irish heritage is at the red rather than the black end of the spectrum. Andy is freckly, strong, on the bins, and married to Sarah, glamorously a bodybuilder (sculptural rather than the hulking kind), who gets to the gym at four in the morning most days, and sells insurance thereafter.

The gathered family – apart from Mandy who was having to endure this on her own, prepping for surgery in a hospital two hundred miles away – meant we had to have a conversation with the nurse overseeing his care. It was time now to take David off ventilation. His death would likely follow, so we talked this through in the family room, over tea which was already coming as steadily and copiously as coal for a locomotive's boiler. I say talked it through; a nurse explained what would happen, and suggested we left the team to their work – I have seen someone have ventilation removed and I understood why – so we talked about nothing consequential, hovering around the reason we were there but not alighting on it, in the way of people on the threshold of inevitable disaster.

Without the tube hanging out of his mouth he seemed more peaceful, although pale and thin, and lying on his back in what looked to me like a Victorian deathbed pose. How unlike him, I thought, to look so composed, who could fall asleep anywhere, in the middle of anything, and did. When we lived in London we once had a team of police officers run through the flat with a helicopter overhead, trying to catch a cat burglar on the rooftops of Belgravia. David, who had nodded off in an armchair, did not stir. He had an unflattering habit of nodding off while I was preaching, and more than once at Evensong, when we all stood for the last hymn, David, in choir dress, would still be 'resting my eyes' while the organ and choir crescendoed, and I would have to step round him to receive the offertory at the altar.

We arranged ourselves around his bed and waited for his breathing to slow and stop.

Mark and his mate Clarkey have come down from Chorley to sort out David's cars. I have one, but David had three: his own car, a Land Rover, and a vintage Morris Minor Cabriolet called Millie. I am embarrassed at my lack of knowledge about cars, so egregious they speak to me slowly and clearly as if I were someone with dementia. It is not that I am particularly stupid, I hope, but because I did not do cars as a teenage boy, nor did I do sport, the latter since rectified. A cliché, but very common in gay men of my age. David too, in spite of sporty brothers, and a father who could fix any car anywhere, was hopeless, to the point that when they went wrong, unless it was absolutely necessary to fix them, they would be abandoned like obsolete tractors in farmyards.

The Land Rover has not run for so long it is being reclaimed by nature. It is beyond salvage, and two men come with a low loader to take it away, a manoeuvre of some difficulty because the steering lock was jammed.

His own car, stuck on the drive since he died, will not start, so they do that thing with jump leads, and it does. I take it out for a drive to get some energy into the battery and some use back into the brakes. When I get in, everything is adjusted to his size and shape and I have to readjust it to mine. It feels very faintly of betrayal so I take the route he used to take to the boat as if each mile on that remembered road would somehow restore the original settings.

Millie I had decided to give to Vinnie, who had overhauled her when she arrived, and sourced parts, and put her back together again after David broke down in her on the M6 with the top stuck down and four dogs in the back. Mark and Clarkey

26

bring a trailer, being practical and capable men, and they push and winch and drive her on, like a reluctant cow going up the ramp to a cattle truck.

As they drive away, I feel for the first time a now frequent anxiety: that he is beginning to fade, and that every day a part of him is less distinct, his voice more distant, his smell, of fags and Jo Malone and whisky, less piquant.

It did not stop.

Evening turned to night, although it was only when I went outside for some fresh air that I noticed it was dark. We had not eaten, or rested, or even paused. David dying was so completely involving, so intense, there was no sense of time passing. And it was so stomach-turningly traumatic I had no appetite, which is exceedingly rare.

Outside it was cold. It was only three days after David's forty-third birthday, the tenth of December, which I had marked by giving him some coffee mugs by our friend the potter Doug Fitch. I thought if I had known it was his last, what would I have done differently? Bought him a Rolex – not that he would have wanted one, but would he have liked the gesture? Whisked him off for a night at Claridge's, which he would have liked without any qualification at all? Or just given him more of my attention than I actually had, because I was tired and Rick Stein was confiting a tomato on television that night?

Pointless speculation, but the action of the cold and being alone outside the hospital made me tremble, and I stood in a corner of the car park, pretending to read the noticeboard as people went to and fro. Some of them recognised me and said hello, but I could not speak, and they looked surprised, and I realised it was because they assumed I was there for profes-sional rather than personal reasons. I remembered making this mistake myself with David once, visiting Tewkesbury Abbey, where I knew the vicar slightly, and there he was finishing a funeral, and I went to say hello and was surprised to see that he was crying, and must have looked surprised, or my tone unsympathetic, for he snapped something and walked away. I looked hard at the hospital map: it showed the location of ICU and all the other wards, and I longed in that moment to have the power, through force of will, to be a bed manager on a computer moving patients round the map, and to pick up David out of ICU and drop him into another ward on the map, so intensive care was scaled down to high dependency, and then down again, and then the discharge suite.

Practical matters. I texted Sarah to update her and to ask if she was able to provide dog care. She was. I texted my curate, Jane, and churchwardens to give them notice that I would need cover for Sunday. The hospital offered us the use of a family room, with a bed and shower en suite, which suited Vinnie and Irene and Mark. We set up camp.

Spiritual matters. I called in at the hospital chapel and said a desperate prayer. It was not a professional prayer, such as I might turn out for a parishioner, something formed and from the kitty of Anglican spirituality. It was, for him, 'please make this go away but I know you are not going to' and, for me, 'I am going to be unavailable for the foreseeable future, please bear with me'. Then I wrote his name on a slip of paper and stuck it on the board alongside all the other names and petitions, asking for everything from a parking space to a miracle (although the former often requires the latter), and went back to ICU.

The Feast of St John of the Cross

David was disinclined to die quickly. Obstinate in life, he was obstinate in dying, and as the hours passed, I needed to make arrangements. I stepped out to do practical things, now and then, like start a WhatsApp group, first response in times of crisis. Sarah, and our neighbour Mel, and Terry, who took care of the construction end of David's projects, volunteered to mind the dogs. We widened the circle of those with bedside rights. Cousins and nephews, and his close and trusted friends were informed. I notified the bishop, who was very kind, and got it just right, but I did not want to tell anyone outside the need-to-know boundary, because I could not have coped with a hundred phone calls, and because, if news got out, I could not have coped with any media interest. I stepped away from social media, a phrase I have had to write infrequently in my life, and hoped if anyone noticed our absence they would think it some sort of Advent discipline.

Stepping back into ICU, in retrospect, was like embarking on a long and sleepless flight to Australia, out of time and space, but with moments that are unusually vivid still. David's extended family, a branch of which is local, came in numbers. My brothers returned with their families, and we arranged ourselves around the bed, moving in and out of the light and the shade, small talk followed by silences, someone suddenly overcome with tears, while Irene and I talked dachshunds.

Dawn came, and I went to the windows, which overlooked a pocket park, just beyond a wooden fence. The rising light revealed a figure fastened to the fence, like the victim of some horrible stag night prank. It was Paddington Bear, slightly larger than the bear we know from books and films, dressed unmistakably in his blue duffel coat and a red shapeless hat and carrying a little suitcase. I guessed there must be some initiative to encourage reading going on, but I did not find the figure encouraging, for his other arm was raised and pointing directly at me. I was unnerved by this. It looked like a *j'accuse*, as if I were responsible for Paddington's indignity, tied to a fence in the cause of children's literature. But I did feel guilty; guilty that I was unable to prevent what was happening, guilty that I did not summon help sooner, guilty that I had not been kinder, guilty that I had not been able to save him. That spiralled quickly, and sucked up the air and grew noisy, like a twister, and I knew I had to let it go.

And then I remembered why the pointing Paddington seemed familiar. He reminded me of a figure in the Grünewald altarpiece, painted five hundred years ago for a monastery at Isenheim which cared for the diseased. It is a crucifixion, and in the panel to the right John the Baptist points to Christ, in terrible extremis, on the cross. It is the same gesture, I realised, as Paddington's, only he was pointing to another man in terrible extremis, my beloved, pale as chalk, in the bed around which we had gathered.

Medics came and went, monitoring, adjusting meds, offering tea, which was always accepted, and I looked at him, sleeping and peaceful, to see signs of decline.

David, being David, produced the opposite. He woke up.

He was groggy, his mouth was dry, his throat sore from the ventilation tube, so it was fluids and mouth care, which he had showed me how to do when my father was dying, in the same hospital, three years before. He was half aware of our presence, but was not sure why he was in hospital.

'Am I dead?' he asked, more than once, curiously rather than anxiously, and he would sometimes wave his arms around, so stuck with needles he reminded me of Saint Sebastian, and complain that his new transplanted hands didn't work properly.

Now I think perhaps he was hoping there was something that could be done, some surgery, or procedure, that could save him, and I feel a stab of guilt again that I did not demand more medical effort be made, because a miracle might have happened, and he would still be alive. Everyone says that is not rational, and they are right, but rational doesn't begin to cover it.

He continued to remain alive, and the urgency of the moment relaxed slightly. As news was carefully disseminated through our immediate circle of friends and relatives, more visitors came. Mo and Bryan, whom we met on pilgrimage in the Holy Land, Roman Catholics, she Irish and to the manner born, he an English convert. I hesitate to stereotype, but Irish Catholics are very good at death. It is part of the culture in a way which seems startling to English middle-class sensibilities. As soon as Mo heard the news she was rattling her rosaries like Carmen her castanets, and they came straight to the hospital. Bryan, bearded in jeans, ex rag trade, white-haired now and retired, took care of material logistics, Mo spiritual. She looks the part, what Miss Jean Brodie might have become had things worked out differently, and is that rare thing, a genuine eccentric, unaware that she is. They live in Rutland, and take care of the dogs when we are away; the first time they obliged I dropped them off with their leads and bowls and food, a bespoke biscuit bought by the costly sackload, but when we returned I discovered that Mo decided that this diet was, to use her word, 'Dickensian', and she fed them what she fed Bryan, even making them individual steak and kidney puddings. This arrangement suited us, them, and most of all the dogs, never dropped off with more anticipation than at theirs.

Terry, David's partner in his various home improvement enterprises, came from work, in his chippy's kit, stocky and short-haired, and slightly ghostly, I thought, until I realised he was filmed with the fine dust of half-built houses. Thomas, David's oldest friend, came from Suffolk. As schoolmates, they'd both been weedy kids, but in maturity Thomas had started going to the gym on the US airbase where both their fathers worked, and is now beefy. He brought with him a husband, Luke, and more of David's backstory: his teenage years in Mildenhall, after he and his parents left the older siblings in Manchester and moved south to new jobs for Vinnie and Irene, and for David a new accent. Original David became more and more overlaid, nursing in hospitals in Bury St Edmunds, then London, Los Angeles and Johannesburg, till the Manchester was so faint it was barely there – until family arrived and then it came back, a long 'a' suddenly short, Antie Kath instead of Aunty Kath.

His niece Steph arrived with her boyfriend Lewis. Steph is tall and blonde, a runner at national level, with that thoroughbred physicality of the athlete. She and David had become close, paddleboarding serenely down at our boat, and we had become friends with both of them. Lewis, also an athlete, is an almost ridiculously broad-shouldered pharmacist at the practice where our dentist has her surgery; in the queue for antibiotics you sense that women, and indeed some men, are queueing in the especial hope that he will be on that day. Steph's younger brother Joey arrived, like Terry still dusty from a building site, but he seems the wrong build for it, more pharmacist than scaffolder, and you wonder, on physique alone, if he and Lewis might not swap jobs. There was a kaleidoscopic quality to David's life, reflected in the sickroom personnel, joined next by Charles and Karen, the Earl and Countess Spencer, stalwart friends and generous hosts at Althorp House, not far from Finedon.

David was conscious when they called, and pleased to see them, and whispered something. I leant in to interpret. 'Kiss me, kiss me,' he said. I kissed him, but he shook his head, crossly. 'TISSUE, TISSUE!' We talked for a while, the niceties of introductions and tactful enquiry fluttering at the edge of a solemn farewell. They said goodbye to David, knowing they would not see him again, and in the instant intimacy of such circumstances, Joey, David's nephew, and Karen embraced, unselfconsciously, with a little puff of powder on contact, hers luxurious and cosmetic, his the unscented dust of stripped plaster.

Charles said, 'Can we take you for a coffee?'

We sat in the Costa next to reception. I am so used to seeing Charles on his territory, behind the protective walls of Althorp and among friends, that I forget how recognisable he is outside it, even though twenty years have passed since his sister's death, and his unforgettable eulogy in Westminster Abbey, watched by half the world. People were looking at us, which happens routinely if they recognise you, or half recognise you, from the television or the papers, but I was so wrapped up in the dynamics of what was happening one floor away that I could not gauge the formalities of that properly. I suppose people were wondering what Princess Diana's brother was doing with the *Strictly* vicar, looking terrible, in the cafe at Kettering General. If this level of curiosity made Charles uncomfortable, he did not show it, nor Karen, who placed a china pail of cappuccino in front of me, and got practical, which she does whenever the going gets tough. What are you going to do? I don't know. What do you need? I don't know. We're here, come and go as you please. Thank you.

We said goodbye and I went back upstairs to ICU. There is a sort of bridge before you get there, connecting the older part of the hospital to the newer, where the ward is, neutral space. I suddenly felt that I was separate from what was happening, floating above it, airborne by caffeine and sleeplessness.

I remembered when I was eighteen I was knocked off my bike. It was in Stratford-upon-Avon, and I was cycling into sixth-form college for a theatre studies lecture on the *Commedia dell'arte*.

My route took me along the Alcester road, one of the main routes into town, at rush hour, and it was busy. I looked behind me, indicated I was pulling out, and made to overtake a row of parked cars; then something peculiar happened.

I was no longer pedalling but still going forward, level with the ground rather than the roofs of the parked cars. *This is odd*, I thought. Then I heard, rather than felt, my knees grating on the road surface. *That's not good*, I thought, as I came to a halt.

There was silence, and it went dark, and then there was a rush of sound and people crowding round me. I tried to get up, but I could not. I felt no pain, no distress, but I knew something had gone badly wrong because I could see it in their faces, and one of them was my flatmate, Joss, who had left home on her bike just after me. She burst into tears. Then I was sick.

The next thing I remember, I was in Stratford's little hospital. Nurses and a doctor were cutting me out of my trousers, a pair of dark blue elephant cords (this was 1980). Blood kept appearing, and the doctor could not work out where it was coming from. Then he saw I had a deep cut on my hand, and when I waved my arms – why was I waving my arms? – I dripped blood like Jackson Pollock dripping paint. 'Will I ever play the cello again?' I said, trying to make light of the injury, and the doctor said, 'Oh, do you play the cello?' 'No,' I said. There was a pause and the doctor said, 'Why did you say you played the cello when you don't?' I tried to think of a reply but gave up. I remember looking at my bloodstained jumper and thinking it looked like Arlecchino's motley, then I felt anxious that I would be late for the lecture. Then I passed out again.

Irene and Vinnie and Mark and I sat shifts at his bedside, as night and day came and went, by now not really distinguishable. Mark and I have always got on well and we got closer, of course, through this extraordinary and exacting time, and he offered to take me to the vicarage for a break, to check on the dogs, to get a change of clothes, to shave and shower, though he was too polite to say why that might be overdue. When we came outside, I saw that it was night and checked my watch – four in the morning – and the only people abroad in such a place at that hour, people to whom very good or very bad things are happening, and the people whose job it is to deal with them. You would think this would encourage a mood of sympathetic generosity, but there was an awkward moment at the car park barrier, when the man on duty said we had the wrong code, given to us by ICU, and tried to charge us more than we owed. If I had been on my own, I don't know how well I would have dealt with this; fortunately, Mark stepped in, with firm grace. The car park man was only doing his job, but someone from ICU leaving a hospital car park at four in the morning is someone you should be given discretion to cut some slack. As a general rule, try not to be impatient with people in hospital car parks. They may be having the worst day of their lives.

At home, the dogs leapt and barked when we came in. Five dachshunds, from a year old to eleven years old, on their own for hours now, apart from visits from the dog rota to let them out and feed them. It was a moment I remember particularly clearly for I saw in them bewilderment and anxiety – was it there, or did I put it there? – but if it was there I would not be surprised, for their routine had been disrupted and their contentment is so contingent on pattern. Seeing what I took to be a reaction in their guileless dogginess pierced me to the heart, for I knew what was happening and they did not, and this disruption was not going to pass, but be permanent.

Permanent. David would not be coming home. The dogs would never see him again. I did not want Mark to see the vicarage, lest it look like a crime scene, and I would be shamed by evidence of the chaos of David's last hours, the bloody tissues, the discarded pharmaceutical packaging, but he made no comment. I had a shower, and in the hot drench woke up to the unfolding tragedy in ICU, and admitted into consciousness a tiny bit more of the brute fact of his dying, and I felt the stomach-twisting pain that every about-to-be-bereaved person feels, of realisation.

Maybe the twist in my stomach provoked a memory of hunger, and on the way back to the hospital we stopped at McDonald's on the bypass, and I tried to eat a burger in horrible lighting next to two wide-awake gamers who had taken a break from their digital campaign for victuals. I don't remember if I actually ate it, if I did it was without any enjoyment. I do remember being very thankful that I was with Mark, who races motorbikes, and has nerve and skill, and is alert for tiny changes, all useful accomplishments to bring to this grim party.

Mark was closest to David in age and affinity, and knew him in both his identities, as a working-class boy from Manchester, and the Oxford-educated clergyman. Both of these identities were adjusted for use by David, and he was sometimes unsettled in both, neither one thing nor the other. I met him in his second identity, his first only became familiar to me over time, and I gradually began to understand better the sources of his insatiable appetite for gravy, his toughness, his fondness for terrible biscuits. These survived his reinvention, a reinvention that began with the move to Suffolk when he was at middle school and lost his Manchester accent to fit in better with the southerners who were now his peers. Like lots of people whose life takes a different direction from their siblings, he was sometimes pulled in opposite directions. When his family was around he would go a bit northern, 'our Dave' rather than David. When he was in his other world he would say he came from Lancashire, which his place of birth, Ashton-under-Lyne, had not been since the formation of Greater Manchester in 1974.

This unsettledness was compounded by being gay. Lots of gay men of our generation had to leave home and hearth to have a liveable life, so reinvention is very common, and it is not uncommon for that reinvention to be partly about culture, or being cultured. A liveable life beyond the horizon of Kettering, where I grew up, was hinted at for me by books, music and painting, for which I hungered and had to go and find for myself. This was true for David too, when he had to find his liveable life, and it was in the County Youth Orchestra, for which he played the violin, and then spells in Italy and France, where he lived and worked and learned the rudiments of the languages, which he spoke with more enthusiasm than accuracy sometimes.

David wore his accomplishments like new clothes (he was a very dressy man), but I think he sometimes felt they were too easily put on and taken off. He looked at my accomplishments, in music and writing and broadcasting, as authentic in a way his weren't; but I only put them on and take them off too, and would sometimes do so competitively, because they conferred on me a prestige, or so I thought, which I did not want to give up or even share. He found the competition wearying, and to keep his head up became absorbed with things I could not compete with – doing places up, knowing about colours, dress, fixing things, crafts. We were at our best together when we were away; away from my career, which dominated everything, away from our overlapping social worlds, mostly in remote parts of Scotland where we went with the dogs every year, Kintyre or Galloway, or Caithness. Far from the madding crowd he would weave wicker and go paddleboarding while I would read and write and cook; and we could go a whole day in each other's exclusive company content, blissfully content, without saying a word.

David had come so far in his forty-three years that Irene sometimes thought he was embarrassed about his background. I don't think he was – on the contrary – but he had reinvented himself, more than once, and like so many who undergo invention and reinvention he was unable to go back, even if he had wanted to.

Mark and I talked a lot about this, in the deathbed hours; about David coming out and finding a new life to lead as a gay man; about him moving to London and finding his feet on his own; and about leaving the Church that his family joined when he was a child (they've since nearly all left). It was what some would call a sect, founded by an American radio evangelist in the thirties, who believed the British and their descendants were the lost tribes of Israel, and so observed the Jewish calendar rather than the Christian calendar, preached the imminent end of the world, required onerous commitment, the stringent observance of rules so marked its critics have described it as a 'doomsday cult'. Among the consequences of this was David's abandonment of his childhood wish to become a dentist, for he believed the Rapture would come before he finished his training and those in the Church would be taken up to heaven, beyond caries, gingivitis and decay. The imminence of the end of the world did not prevent the founder from building lavishly in Pasadena, most splendid among his works the auditorium now home to that city's Symphony Orchestra. To fund these he exacted a tithe on members, three times a year, which must have fallen very heavily on Vinnie and Irene, raising a family of six on Vinnie's wage.

David was a little boy when the family joined. His most vivid memory of this was getting very excited at the sight of his parents taking down the Christmas decorations, only to see them thrown out rather than hung up. Christmas was, for the duration of their membership, cancelled, so when Christmas was restored he kept it with zeal. The vicarage at Finedon was transformed into a cross between Sandringham and Santa's Grotto on the first day of December every year. For David it never lost its magic – unusual for a clergyman. His excitement and pleasure when it came around was infectiously charming, and he was for me especially lovable as the great feast approached. I remember one year, after Midnight

Mass, I put the dogs' Christmas stockings up on the fireplace and he scolded me for doing it in front of them and spoiling the surprise.

Vinnie and Irene told me he had been a trusting and loving child, and when he was a baby he was always smiling, so my nickname for him was Smiler. Recalling this at his deathbed, as the Christmas decorations went up around us, for a celebration that he was not going to see, was almost unbearably painful, and twice I have had to stop writing this paragraph.

When your partner dies they take with them your future. David and I had always planned to get a little house in the west of Scotland, Kintyre or maybe Galloway, there to spend our days wearing jumpers he had knitted and eating kippers I had smoked, playing the fiddle and the accordion in the local ceilidh band, helping out at a tiny Episcopalian church. We had started to turn this into reality, looking at houses, talking to people we know who lived in the places we liked, and the nearer it came to becoming reality, the more detailed the imagined future became.

And now it has all gone, and when I look ahead I see nothing. A friend of mine who skippers a lifeboat once took the helm of an icebreaker in the Gulf of Bothnia at the invitation of the captain but found it impossible to get his bearings, because everything he saw out of the window was undifferentiated white, ice meeting sky with an invisible join. The captain showed him the satellite chart of the ship's movements and it was all over the place. In spite of instruments telling him where he was, his internal instruments spun like a weathervane in a typhoon. That's how it felt when I looked forward.

*

My brother Will also took me out one night. I decided I

needed to get some milk, or whisky, or another essential – why this should occur to me at midnight I don't know – so we went in his car to the late shop on the edge of Kettering town centre. It was surprisingly busy, with people who use late shops at midnight, queueing at the till for drink, tobacco and Rizlas. I fell into conversation with someone who was perhaps at the edge of respectable society and I could see Will was a little uneasy that I was talking to him, although he was perfectly pleasant. And then I realised Will was not concerned about him, but about me, and that interacting with someone outside our intimate, intense circle was revealing my volatility rather than his.

Another trip out with Mark seems bizarre, in retrospect, but made perfect sense at the time. We drove one afternoon to the village near Kettering where my brother Will lives, partly to see him and family, but also to pay a visit to the church so I could show Mark where David would be buried, me too, when required.

A few years ago, David mentioned at supper that he had bought our graves. He had arranged for an application to be made to the Parish Church Council that he and I might be buried in adjacent graves in the churchyard in the village where we have a cottage. It had not occurred to me to think that far forward, and I must have looked surprised because he quickly said this was 'a northern thing' and perfectly normal. Mark was surprised too when I told him this. It was not a northern thing that he had ever heard of, and I wonder now if David was, as usual, pretending something remarkable was unremarkable, a technique he often used when he was involving me in decision-making after the fact. I wonder if he was not also foreseeing his need for this earthy accommodation arising earlier than expected. A site visit was arranged and I met the churchwardens to pick the spot. David was, as usual, late; so late that by the time he arrived they had departed and I had chosen the plot alone, on the unfashionable north side of the churchyard, in a tight space between the chancel and the vicarage wall, a suitably humble spot for two priests, mindful that the last should be first and the first should be last. David did not appreciate this nicety on my part, arguing that there were brighter spots with better views, despite my argument that not only was the humble spot suitable, but the view would not be something readily to captivate us from six feet under. It seemed then its occupancy would be a remote possibility, but here we were, looking at the even and untroubled turf that would soon be lifted so that he could go in.

Back at the hospital, another visit, this time from the Bishop of Brixworth. David, a traditionalist in many ways, was far from traditional in his attitude to bishops. In spite of a slightly renegade reputation, and a life outside the Church, I was formed in an ecclesial culture which considers obedience to the authority of bishops a high priority, at least 'in all things lawful and honest' as the promises we make at our ordination require. David, who had been running occupational health for a large company before ordination, took a different view, and was sometimes rather a turbulent and strategic priest where authority was involved. Consequently his relationship with the bishops was occasionally problematic and I wondered if they might have felt some apprehension about approaching him on his deathbed, when his mindfulness of the proprieties was even less lively. If that was the case, the bishop did not show it. We talked in the relatives' room and then I took him through to see David, with his parents and Mark and Terry and me round his bed.

The bishop produced the holy oil for anointing the sick. David was not conscious, and we sat in silence as the bishop made the sign of the cross with it on his forehead. There's a beautiful prayer said when the dying person is anointed:

Go forth upon your journey from this world,
in the name of God the Father Almighty who created you;
in the name of Jesus Christ who suffered death for you;
in the name of the Holy Spirit who strengthens you;
in communion with the blessed saints,
and aided by angels and archangels,
and all the armies of the heavenly host.
May your portion this day be in peace,
and your dwelling the heavenly Jerusalem.
Amen.

We all sat in silent tears.

If you ever wonder what the relevance of the Christian faith might be for people today, try a deathbed. It was a beautiful and important moment, for it created a moment and a space for full awareness of what was happening to David, that he was going from us, the hard fact that we shy away from, medicalised or palliated in some other way, but we need to know. It also – but this is a separate thing – points to a horizon beyond that, over the threshold of this world where the mystery of God awaits. To many that may seem the palliative, but it is not. It only works because we know this is the end, and that the person we love will go from us, never to return – gone into the next room, in the words of that overworked funeral reading, but a room separated from us by an unbridgeable chasm. You have to die in order to inherit eternal life; not seeming death but the real thing.

And then David woke up. He opened his eyes to see the bishop in front of him, with an oily thumb aloft. He seemed to have trouble focusing and the bishop said, 'David, can you see me?' David said, 'I can see . . .' and then there was a pause and he seemed to look at us gathered round, '. . . a flight of angels?'

I think if he could have winked, he would have.

Martin arrives at the vicarage. He stands in the doorway and says 'Darlin' . . .' and extends his arms and we embrace. I feel myself emit a little sob, like a fart unintentionally released at the gym. Martin is my friend in Scotland, with whom I stay when I am up for the Edinburgh Festival, and have for nearly thirty years now. We met when I was dating his friend Russell, a comrade from seventies Clydeside communism, and after Russell died of AIDS in the nineties we became closer. He stands back. 'You look terrible.' He looks fantastic, ten years older than me, but in better shape in his sixties than I was in my thirties. He trains at a kickboxing gym with Poles forty years younger, dresses with effortless style, and stands out everywhere, half Glaswegian, half Métis, the son of a Canadian ice hockey professional who got lonely on a tour of Scotland in the fifties. He had his DNA done a while ago and I now parse in his face the complex heritage that is his: Pictish, French, Cree, and then some. He was en route to Australia when David died and did not get back until after the funeral. And now he is here, on a mission to comfort me and fix the chaos which he knows lies beyond the doors I have closed on David's last weeks and months. He is a working-class Glaswegian of the fifties, who regards untidiness and uncleanliness as moral dereliction, and he has no poker face, and his distaste for what he sees is obvious, but so is his relish for the task.

He calls Jo, one of my parishioners, and his friend, and she arrives with a bale of black bin liners and yellow Marigold gloves. Together they go in. I sit at the dining room table going through piles of documents while Martin and Jo go up and downstairs, taking some bags to the tip, others to the Salvation Army. Martin is impatient with my anxiety over triage, that I must approve the disposal of all things lest something go that I later regret. And I yield, because I know that I do not want to get rid of anything, and at the same time that I want to get rid of everything. I cannot make those judgements, so Martin makes them instead. In the clear-out I lost only one thing I later looked for, something of indiscernible sentimental value that would not have passed the later triage which came when Mark and Terry cleared the garage, filling two skips.

Even Martin, in his purifying zeal, does not dispose of a box he found of photographs, which I have never seen before, of David as a child and youth and a young man, dozens of them. I do not know why David had not shown them to me, but they are heartbreaking to look at now. There is one of him and his two brothers, taken nearly forty years ago, underexposed and badly composed and printed on a glossy white-bordered square. He must have been about five, so sweet and affectionate, holding Ralph, his stuffed rabbit. Why is it so affecting? Because he is innocent of what is to come, the shadow that fell across his life and shortened it and took him away.

The Raising of Lazarus

That night, at the hospital, Vinnie and Irene and Mark and I took turns to sit with him. Then nurses produced a sort of lounger hospital chair which we put next to his bed. I relieved Irene of duty sometime in the small hours, and pulled a blanket over myself in the soft medical light and listened to his breathing, which sent me to sleep. I woke up after a couple of hours and for a blissful second or two did not know where I was. I looked at the blanket, which was half hanging off my knees, and my socked feet, and the unfamiliar chair. And then I remembered where I was and what was happening. It is the worst moment, when you realise what you have woken up to, the opposite of that feeling of immense relief when you wake from a nightmare, then remember it is not real. This is the nightmare you wake into. I looked at David, sleeping, and my stomach suddenly twisted again, and I knew, in that moment, that I was losing him. David was dying. Soon he would no longer be here, and I would be alone. That sudden shift, unprotected by the buffers consciousness erects between us and data too horrible to handle, shifted the jumble of what I was feeling, a mixture of denial and anger and curiosity, and as it tumbled away, sorrow filled the space, sorrow of an intensity I had not experienced before. And then it was gone, as wakefulness grew in strength, and the defences went up again.

Another night, another day. Mel, our neighbour, sent me a picture on the WhatsApp group of our dogs playing in their garden with her kids, a scene of middle-class contentment on the lawn of the old vicarage, my church in the background, that was comforting beheld from the crisis I was in. Kate, my PA, was in daily contact. She not only knows what I want people to know, she knows what I don't want people to know, especially me, and anticipates my unspoken anxieties without saying anything, and deftly reassured me that I need not worry about letting anyone down, or missing a deadline, and that all discretion will be observed, and I need not worry.

I did worry. I worried about the dogs and about work, because I could. I did not worry about David because it would make no difference, at least at first. As the clock ticked and he held on to life I wondered if the hospital would need the ICU bed back. We could not possibly make a case for holding on to it if someone needed it to get better, and I asked to be talked through what would happen in that event. David would be moved to a side room on a ward. If that had to be, then we would have to live with it, but there would be no family room available for Vinnie and Irene and Mark, with a bed and shower and a loo, and that would be difficult. I asked again if they would let me get them a room at the hotel down the road, so they could at least take time out for a sleep and a shower, but Irene said she would not be going anywhere. Then I thought what about the local hospice, where there was room for families to be accommodated? But it was felt David would not survive a transfer.

He was sinking, and then he would rally, and then he would sink again. He was on morphine, provided by a driver that gave a measured dose automatically, and if he showed any signs of distress the dose could be gradually increased. Occasionally he would groan, or try to move, and sometimes he would speak and hold a slightly weird conversation. I realised that the opportunity for him and me to say any more than we already had said was limited, so when he was more or less conscious I asked to be left alone with him. I got onto the bed and held him as gently as I could, and told him I loved him and he had brought gifts and goods, and frustration and testing, that I had never imagined would come my way, and I was so grateful for him, and then I stroked his hair and sang him 'A Case of You'. I don't know if David heard what I said, or knew what it meant, but I did know that he loved me and that I loved him, and that nothing could have separated us apart from what was separating us, so I did not fret too much about leaving anything unsaid.

After a while my brother came in and said, 'Christ, Tricky, your belly,' and I saw that I had overspilled my belt, and that most intense of moments ended with me thinking, *I must try the 5/2 diet.*

David's diet was 7/7 on end-of-life care, but because he took longer to die than expected he began to thirst, so the medics put him on a drip to get some fluids into him. I was at first quite disturbed by this because I thought it might prolong his dying and I wanted it to be over, for his sake and for ours. I have found that when someone is dying the convenience of others, denied at first, becomes a more powerful factor in deciding what to do and what not to do, as the hours become days. Certainly our needs grew more insistent, for food and drink and showers and rest. There were moments when it seemed he was about to die, but then he would come back. Eventually the pattern altered, he was no longer conscious, and his face discoloured, a dark bruise like a shadow spreading almost visibly. His breathing changed and one of the nurses explained that was the body approaching shut down, Cheyne-Stokes breathing, and that death would not be long in coming. More hours went by and he seemed to be restless, and I thought perhaps agitated. I asked the nurse if she could up the dose, but I think by then he was probably on the maximum. He grew calm again, and settled again, and we went back to the long routine.

I said to Mark I was going to nip home and check on the dogs. It was about two in the morning. The dogs were oblivious of the hour, just pleased to see me, and I made a cup of tea and sat down for five minutes with them on the sofa, and closed my eyes. The next thing I knew my phone was ringing. It was five in the morning, and it was Mark.

'He's gone.'

Another variation on the theme of grief comes from time to time as the weeks become months. The piercing grief is less frequent but in its place is an occasional visit from cold, stony grief, that comes up from depths. The other day I was driving through a town somewhere, down a street of terraced Victorian houses, red brick, and there was something about their blank gaze, at the street and at each other, that admitted this feeling. The houses to me seemed to be saying, 'You will never be happy again, you will never be happy again,' like a bench of judges passing sentence on a convicted malefactor, me.

I don't remember driving to the hospital, but I remember arriving in David's room. Irene and Vinnie were at his bed-side, and Mark too, and David was lying tidily on the bed, his eyes half-closed, in the unmistakable stillness of death. Unmistakable, but in need of certification by a competent authority, and as we sat and talked a doctor arrived and per-formed, with professional detachment, the necessary tests.

Vinnie, not a demonstrative person, was crying. Irene and Mark and I talked about what we were going to do. And then Mark erupted into sobs.

I don't think I cried at that moment. I stroked David's hair and kissed him on the forehead, expecting the chill of death, but the body was not cold. Still, and room temperature, chambré – and that is the shock, for the body in life, even if only a thread of life, is animated, pulsing, vital, and warm.

It was by now after seven in the morning and I decided I would tweet the news of David's death. I asked the others first if that was OK with them, and they said yes. I wanted to let people know, but I could not face a hundred phone calls, and I did not want people to find out from another source. So I tweeted a picture of us both, on the Mount of Olives in our dog collars, when we were leading a pilgrimage to the Holy Land, and said that I was sorry to say that he had died, and that he had been ill for some time. I added a line from Isaiah: 'the Lord shall be thine everlasting light, and the days of thy mourning shall be ended.'

I said, pompously, 'I'm going to press send,' as if it were an announcement from Buckingham Palace, but I was sending David's death out into the world, and there could be no recall. I pressed send, and thought of a dead Viking on a burning ship heading towards the horizon.

The sister took me to one side and gave me a leaflet. It was a 'what to do when someone dies' leaflet, a genre I came to know well. They often have a picture on the front of a dandelion clock fretted by the wind, its seeds airborne, to soothe the recipient. And inside, what I was looking for: the information about what came next. 'Don't do this now,' she said, and invited us to sit with his body for as long as we wanted, but I knew from other deathbeds that post-mortem processes, physical and administrative, were already under-way, and I needed suddenly to get out of there.

We sat in the family room for the last time, over the last cup of tea, and worked out what to do. Irene and Vinnie said they were going to drive home, desperate for the dog and their own bed, and their own space. Mark said he would head for home too, but would see me sorted first. My brother Will arrived and was given the job of finding somewhere for breakfast, for I thought, in the shock of the moment, that eating something substantial would be a good idea. My father, who thought the best cure for a high fever was two Weetabix, would have been proud.

I said goodbye to Vinnie and Irene, in all of us a desire to get home and collect ourselves, and do the laundry, and the shopping, and be surrounded by the comforts of familiarity, at war with the desire, the need, to be together. It was over. The vigil, in which we had grown so close, and held on to David so tenderly, so lovingly, was done, and he was gone, and it was time for us to go too.

Will booked us a table at the hotel on the bypass, over-looking the McDonald's where Mark and I had eaten without appetite a night or two before, and we sat in its dining room chewing on meaty sausages and crispy bacon and fried bread, the Full English Breakfast, which seemed right for the solemnity of the occasion, but it fell into my empty stom-ach like a cow down a well, and lay there, indigestibly. My phone purred and pinged, and I looked at it to see the first messages of condolence arrive. I also noticed others in the dining room looking at us; whether that was because they recognised me, or had seen the news, which disseminated at the speed of touch-typing through social media and then the news media, or if we just looked like we had been in mortal combat and were wreathed in it, like bad aftershave.

I said goodbye to Mark, a wrench, for he had become, in these four days, like a brother to me. And then Will, my biological brother, took me back to his, where Julia made me a coffee, and I sprawled on the sofa as his children came downstairs with condolences. I then decided to go home, and Will came with me to make sure I was OK, although I thought I was OK.

I wasn't OK.

I stopped at the Co-op in Thrapston to pick up some essentials: bread, milk, cheese, tomatoes. But when I came out, I looked in my shopping bag and saw that I had bought three kinds of Parmesan, in a block, grated, and the ersatz kind in a cardboard drum which lasts for years and I secretly like, even though it tastes like stale vomit.

Then I badly wanted to be alone. I had spent hardly any time on my own, or at home, for the past four days, and I longed to get back, to have a shower, to lie on the sofa with the dogs, watch television, and eat something.

I thought that was what I wanted, but it was not. I did not know what I wanted to do because I had just been blown up. A friend of mine, a priest, was first on the scene after Scott's restaurant in Mayfair was bombed by the IRA in the seventies. As the dead and dying lay in blood and broken glass, a couple sitting at a table were calmly eating their dinner and making small talk, although most of their clothes had been blown off in the blast. In shock we repeat the repertoire of the everyday.

I said goodbye to Will and came home, but it was a Tuesday morning and Sarah and Lisa, who look after the vicarage, were in doing their thing. They were so kind and gentle with me, they were both close to David, and had been on the inside of the drama of his failing health, but I wanted to be alone with the dogs, to tell them what had happened and to reassure them that things would be OK. Irrational, but necessary. I went to our bedroom and they followed, and I lay on the bed and they jumped all over me, and licked me, and sniffed me, giving their version of reassurance. I hugged them, and held them up, so we were face to face, one by one, and I did not tell them in words what had happened, but it did feel necessary to look at them and for them to look at me. If I could have talked to them, I don't know what I would have said – 'It will be OK'?

The cliché of gay couples substituting ornamental dogs for children is long and noble, and while I could not quite claim that we looked on ours as the sons and daughters we did not have, they were part of our household and at the centre of our lives. Daisy came first, the gift of an eccentric millionaire whom I met once, but he saw in my life a gap that could be filled only by a dog. 'OK, yeah,' I said, and thought no more about it, until his PA phoned to tell us that a car would pick up David – we were living in Knightsbridge at the time – and take him to the Randolph Hotel in Oxford. There a breeder would hand over Daisy, and then the car would take David and Daisy to meet me and the eccentric millionaire at Pet Kingdom in Harrods, where he kitted her out with, among other things, a shampoo which cost four times what I paid for mine.

We then moved to Norfolk when David became curate at Wymondham Abbey, and there Daisy was joined by Pongo, her nephew. And then when I became vicar we moved to Finedon, where we were joined by Audrey, then H, then finally General Guster – the last two David's unauthorised additions. I would have stopped at three, but he would have happily had a dozen. Five dachshunds looked after by two people, one often away, is difficult enough, but on my own I simply would not be able to take proper care of them. I knew this from the past few days, when they had been left at home alone for long periods in the care of helpful friends and neighbours, but it was not the same.

They had not been out, apart from the neighbours' garden, in days, so Lisa suggested I take them for a walk; good for them, good for me too. I took their leads from the hook by the front door – when they realised what was happening they howled with excitement and ran in circles at my feet – and I loaded them into the car and drove to a village nearby. It's a very pretty village, on a bend in the river Nene, and you can walk there without seeing anyone else, with the dogs off their leads, and there is a pub for lunch which is so like the ideal of an English country pub you start looking for the cameras. David and I went there often on my day off, and it had become special to us, the nearest place to the parish where we could be far enough away and together enough, with just the dogs, doing what we liked doing best – nothing.

I shepherded them, rather than led them, across a little wooden footbridge at the mill race, and into the fields beyond. I had only gone twenty yards when I realised it was a mistake. Daisy, our oldest dog, who was always David's dog and pack leader, kept stopping and looking behind her, looking for him. Dogs have no guile, or their tells are so obvious – the wagging tail – that they would make the worst poker players imaginable. And they have no tact, so there was no attempt to pretend everything was OK. People pretend everything is OK, you have to sometimes, to get through the inescapable responsibilities of the day; but not dogs. She got more distressed, and more determined not to go further without him, and I gave up, and stood by the river. Cry me a river, I thought, I cried a river over you.

I got them back in the car and went home, and sat at my desk in my study, wondering what to do next. Sarah and

Lisa appeared and asked me if I was all right. I was not, and I trembled while my social apparatus – eyes, mouth, hands – tried to continue conversing coherently. They sat with me, kind and patient, until that squall had passed.

I tried to pray, and saw that in Cuba today, 17 December, it is the Feast of the Raising of Lazarus. It happens on a different day in most other places, but in Cuba there is a big procession to a church with a miraculous icon depicting this event, when Jesus goes to Bethany, the home of Mary and Martha, who are mourning the death of their brother Lazarus, now lying in his tomb. Martha knows enough of Jesus, the mystery of his identity, to be angry with him – if he had come earlier, he could have saved him. I am the resurrection and the life, says Jesus, and at his command Lazarus emerges, wrapped in his grave clothes, but alive again. It prefigures Jesus's own resurrection, his victory over the grave, a triumph in which we all share, but I could not bring myself to say alleluia. I could not get past Martha's anger.

I decided to check in with the outside world. Twitter and Facebook, to which I had uploaded the same notice, were filling with comments, too many to look at, so I went to texts, the medium through which family and closest friends communicate. At the head of the list was a text from my oldest friend, Matthew, whom I grew up with, and now lives in Devon with his wife and their children, themselves grown up now, and his parents and sisters and nephews and nieces all nearby, like the Waltons on their mountain. I have always associated Matthew with the sort of solid, tribal care that characterises his family, and I wanted some of that. I called him and he answered in the level tone I like so much, and needed to hear, because he has answered with it so many times in the adventures and misadventures of a fifty-year friendship.

Then I called Lorna, who I met in 1980 in a queue which she had caused at West Hampstead Tube station looking for coppers to make her fare in a purse produced from the pocket of the dungarees she invariably wore then, and would not wear for gardening now. The queue's irritation made me feel protective towards her, and we have been feeling protective of each other ever since, as flatmates within a year of that first meeting, as artist and manager in the Communards, and then sharing a London house in the nineties. Forty years went by, and she is now a tycoon, dresses like a very chic hotel, but her high cheekbones and freckles and grey blue eyes, the inheritance of Eire, have not changed. Nor has her voice.

'Come down,' she said. 'Come down next weekend.'

Martin texted me from Glasgow airport, waiting to depart for Australia, where he would be until after New Year. 'When I get back, I'll pick up a change of clothes and come straight down.' 'Are you sure?' 'Of course I'm sure. See you after Hogmanay.'

New Year was coming, but before that, Christmas. What was I going to do? I knew what I was not going to do. I was due to lead an outdoor carol service at the retail park the following day, but even in shock I knew I would not be able to manage that. Christmas Day was a week away, but I knew I could not face the candlelit crib at midnight, and the carols we had first sung when we were children ourselves. I called Jane, my curate, and she was already on it, cover was arranged, and I was not to worry about it for a moment.

The phone went. It was the bishop. 'Don't think about work. Take as much compassionate leave as you like. We'll sort out cover.' Everyone assured me of their prayers. There was a ring on the doorbell. It was my neighbour, Hugh, with condolences. The doorbell rang several times more, and in the end I retreated to the sitting room and put on the television and watched it without interest and ate something from the freezer without appetite and had a bath and drank two whiskies, and worried I would not be able to sleep, took half a sleeping pill from David's stash, and went to bed.

The dogs filled the vacant half, but had for a while since David's restless leg syndrome became so athletic he had made camp in a guest room to spare us a nocturnal kicking. At its worst, it was like sharing a bed with Diversity, and it became impossible for me and for the dogs, but I missed his presence next to me, and falling asleep and waking up next to him. Never again, and I realised I could not remember the last time we had gone to bed together and woken up together. My first night of widowhood, and I was glad of the dogs, two on, three in, close to me as I fell asleep, in a fog of fatigue and soporifics, to the sound of Daisy snoring, which sounded soothingly like David's snoring.

I saw a cartoon once in a magazine which showed people arriving at the gates of hell, damned to an eternity of torture. The devil welcomed them by handing each an accordion. A parishioner gives me mine, it was played by her husband, who we buried a while ago. 'You have it,' she said, when I told her how much I liked it when he played. I take it home – heave it, more like, they are heavier than they look, lacquered boxes containing half a piano, half an organ, a canteen of cutlery, and a tiny wind farm.

The half a piano is all right, I know my way round that; the button side and the bellows is another matter, and I get a teacher, Janis, a local man with Latvian heritage. He is a master, and makes it look as easy as breathing, because that is what 100,000 hours of practice does. For a novice it is like playing the mouth organ on a pec deck while working a cash register.

He is patient, and explains clearly what I need to do, and in a couple of weeks I can produce a recognisable, if menacing, 'My Bonnie Lies Over the Ocean'. I say I like Scottish music and at the next lesson Janis produces 'Ye Banks and Braes o' Bonnie Doon'. 'Do you know it?' Yes, I do, David and I used to play it, him on the fiddle, me on the piano, it was one of our party pieces, but I do not tell him this.

Learning to play an old tune on a new instrument; steps that I climb slowly, like a G-major scale on the bass buttons.

I had made myself think, last thing, that I was a widow, and to wake with that knowledge secure, so I would not have to suffer another bereavement as consciousness bloomed. It did not work. I woke, and for a second was in the prelapsarian world of coupledom, and then remembered, and my stomach twisted again.

I got up, and let the dogs out, and said Morning Prayer, which had a healing miracle in the New Testament reading, and I found I could not go on with it. I needed to deal with this-world rather than next-world. The Christian hope of life beyond death seemed suddenly rather abstract, and so I had decided to start the admin, which is mountainous, I knew from experience, and from the instructions in the death leaflet, which requested I visit, at my earliest convenience, the Bereavement Office in the hospital. I dreaded the thought of having to deal with the car park again rather than the bureaucracy of David's death.

I took the dogs out for a short and chaotic walk along a lane, mercifully deserted, and as soon as I could I went to the retail park at Rushden Lakes, where I had been due to host the carol service that night. I went to buy gifts, lavish gifts of luxury hand cream from L'Occitane for the nurses in ICU. David told me that what nurses really want is not chocolates or flowers but hand cream, due to the chapping nature of their calling, and I was so grateful for their care of David and the rest of us that I thought I would treat them to the best I could find.

It was early, just after opening time, and there were not many people about but a woman, well dressed, stopped me and said, 'I'm so sorry to hear your news.' I thanked her, and she told me that she was a widow too. Tears came to my eyes and she took my arm. 'I know, I know.' 'What do *I* need to know?' I asked. She thought about that for a moment and said, 'People will never be as nice to you again as now, so get the most out of it.' It made me laugh.

Two security guards came to say hello, and said they were looking forward to the carol service later. I did not want to have to explain why I would not be there, so I just nodded, and we made small talk, and then one said he was sorry to see my news, and I crumpled a bit.

I checked my phone and saw that David's death had been reported on the news websites. I looked at Twitter and saw that I was trending, not far behind the impeachment hearing of Donald Trump. How David would have liked that. Facebook was filling up, too many messages to answer, but I was glad to see them. Grief is isolating, and to know that others have noticed, and want you to know, was helpful.

I went to Kettering General, found a parking space, and returned to ICU, feeling faintly like the old boy going back to school where he no longer has the standing he once did, and is slightly surprised to see the place managing perfectly well without him. I saw one of the sisters and handed over the bag, heavy with unguents rich in shea butter and verbena and almond. She asked how I was doing, and I said, 'I don't really know.' 'You won't,' she said, 'but be kind to yourself.' I wonder now if she saw what was coming, but had not yet arrived, the questions that come when you are untimely bereaved. Could I have done more? Could I have prevented this? Could I have been kinder, not to myself but to him? These pressed at the edge of consciousness, like shoppers at Harrods' door on the first morning of the sales, but I was not admitting them yet.

On the ship today three times I am asked by passengers we had met who've not heard the news, so I tell them, and they are kind, but everyone flinches at making a faux pas, and at death stepping, trespassing, into their day a little bit. At first you feel like the Ancient Mariner when this happens, but you get used to it. Actually, cruise ships provide as sympathetic an environment as can be, popular with widows old and new. We have one on board: a ninety-year-old with an Ancient Mariner beard and tales of an extraordinary life. Unlike the literary mariner, he is full of beans, and sits in an advantageous spot on deck outside the Persimmon Lounge to sing his siren song to any passing widow. He is so amorous he is known as Handy Andy, I discover from an octogenarian whom he took to watch Sunset Boulevard, *and got frisky and squeezed her knee during Norma Desmond's staircase descent. What did you do? I asked. 'I said, "For fuck's sake, do I look like a teenager?"' Then she added, 'Sorry, Vicar, I'm from London.'*

After visiting ICU I began the process of admin, or sadmin as I came to call it: the post-mortem bureaucracy which grinds exceeding small and can be so long you start to feel it will outlast grief.

It begins in the Bereavement Office. At Kettering General it is quite an expedition to get there, at some distance from the new and bespoke ICU in what feels like a slightly improvised part of its sprawl, one of the shanty town departments so often found in hard-pressed NHS estates. On the way I saw Roger the Sausage's 'parents', as dog owners say, and they offered me condolences, and I guessed that I should offer mine too. I was right, they too had an appointment with the Bereavement Office.

I checked in and someone invited me into another room done out in soothing blond wood, with upholstered chairs, and boxes of tissues ready to blot the freshly rising tears of grief. At Kettering it is run by my beloved cousin Judy, who came down to see me when I got there. Her sister, my equally beloved cousin Kate, had died in her forties too; I had taken the funeral, and now here we were again with another untimely death.

I was glad to see her, it softened the process, the blunt realities of data capture, registration, sign-off, duties assigned to another member of staff, who sat with me. Turning death into bureaucracy is like being in court, when the mess of human misadventure is rationalised, set out, explained, contentiously, by processes which look dispassionate but are not always dispassionate, because no human activity ever is. She was kind and patient, and explained what the details were, and what they meant. For the first time I saw on the Cause of Death notification 'GI bleed'; gastro-intestinal, an unusual perforation of the oesophagus, apparently, but I was not really interested in that because I could not get past the typing.

There was David's name, his DOB, 10.12.76, and now his DOD, 17.12.19, official, and I thought of his headstone with the same data carved on, impressed into the record, beyond negotiation or quibble. There was another form, for the funeral directors.

Had I thought of anyone?

Yes, I would use the firm I work with all the time, local to

Finedon, an excellent family business run by two brothers, one in the office, a familiar but disembodied voice to me, and one who runs ops, who I see all the time and who has become a friend. There is a form for them as well, which, once filled, allows them to come and collect the body from 'Rose Cottage', hospital euphemism for the mortuary, and take it to their place, to lie in a cold room until the funeral. The pressure is sometimes on, especially in winter, in times of flu, when Rose Cottage can fill up very quickly, so while no one pressurises you into expediting this, the bereaved are encouraged to make contact as soon as possible, unless there is a question about the cause of death, when a different procedure applies, involving a post-mortem and an inquest. David's death was not mysterious. If it had been, his body would be the property of the Crown, and the business of the coroner, who has to release it for burial or cremation once all necessary inquiries are completed. I once had a funeral where the body was not released for six months because a cause of death could not be determined (it turned out to be water poisoning). A gap of six months between death and burial was very difficult, particularly because the young woman died a week before her wedding. She was buried in her wedding dress, to the hymns they had chosen for rejoicing, not lamentation. That may sound jarring, but rejoicing and lamentation often come together, and Christianity gets this. One of my favourite funeral prayers, the Russian Kontakion for the Departed, is explicit:

Give rest, O Christ, to thy servant with thy saints:
where sorrow and pain are no more;
neither sighing but life everlasting.
Thou only art immortal, the creator and maker of man:
and we are mortal, formed from the dust of the earth,

and unto earth shall we return:
for so thou didst ordain,
when thou created me, saying:
'Dust thou art und unto dust shalt thou return.'
All we go down to the dust;
and weeping o'er the grave we make our song:
Alleluia, alleluia, alleluia.

We used to sing this at the funeral of the monks of the monastery where I trained for the priesthood. As the coffin was wheeled out of the church to the calvary, the monks' graveyard, we would sing it from the organ loft, disembodied male voices, and it is powerful stuff indeed when the Christian community gathers to see into the earth, and into eternity, one of their own.

But I could take no comfort in that, in the prose of bereavement bureaucracy, in the blond wood environment of the grief-stricken, holding my bits of paper, and forms, and leaflets.

I made an appointment to see the funeral directors, Jonathan and Michael, the following day, and another online to see the registrar, whom I discovered resides in Kettering library, between large-print fiction and the art gallery devoted to Kettering's most celebrated son, and went to see my mum.

Widowhood in lockdown and I am alone at home and have to do gardening and housework, chores outsourced till now. I clean a kitchen counter using an unguent in a spray bottle, and stand and admire my work for ten minutes, then, exhausted, sit in the garden. Then I water some plants and deftly cut back some straggling tendrils of what I think may be a honeysuckle. I sit down again and think how much of David's life was taken up with doing these things so that I could do my things, and how little I understood and appreciated it.

Best of all, in this enforced solitude, is the garden, for it was David's domain, his joy, his canvas, and is now his continuing presence, for what he planted is coming up, and every day it is like he has brought me a bunch of flowers, and set me a technical challenge, so I do not have to plunder the finite resource of memory to be with him.

Mum lives in a village a few miles from Finedon, is chair and bed bound and looked after by carers. She also has dementia, fortunately mild, but sometimes she is more fully aware than at others, and sometimes she confuses me for her brother and frets that we, her fifty-something children, have not had their tea or their baths or been put to bed. Passing on information about deaths, which happens not infrequently with octogenarians, is hit and miss, and you never know if the data is going to land in a part of consciousness capable of retaining it. Will had been to see her and told her the news, but I had to go and see her too, but I was not sure if I could face explaining more than once that David had died. For the same reason, I was on transmit rather than receive on social media. I could not possibly thank everyone for their condolences, and did not want to get into a conversation with anyone other than family and friends, the friends who knew about the state of David's health.

Mum was having a good day, and fully aware of what had happened, so I was spared. Instead we discussed, with typical lack of sentimentality on her part, our separate but similar states of widowhood. Hers had been prepared for, because my father, who died in 2016, had Parkinson's, so his death was preceded by a long and slow decline, which eventually obliged admission to a nursing home. The last year of his life he was so debilitated she called it her widow practice. 'But nothing really prepares you for it when it happens. Worst thing is coming home to an empty house on a dark night.' She looked to her right, to the chair, souped up and capable of lifting and reclining, identical to hers, save the colour, where my father used to sit, both facing the television, which became in his debilitated and her burdened state, the least unbearable thing.

I looked too at my father's empty chair. For more than eighty years he had walked around, picked things up, put them down, hummed, forgotten his hat, avoided people, mowed the lawn, fought Communists, listened to Bruckner, and sat in chairs in which he sat no longer. The thought now of David not sitting in a chair, not humming, not making pastry, not driving badly, not playing the violin, not tackling violent drunks, not planting sweet peas, was in that moment unbearable. In an instant I realised that my future was emptied without him in it, and I thought of a picture made of coloured sand and the wind blowing the sand away leaving no trace of what was there before.

'What will you do for Christmas?' Mum asked.

I said I did not know, I had not thought about it yet.

'When *is* Christmas?'

'It's next week.'

I remembered my grandmother's last Christmas. She was a hundred and one, and living in a nursing home, barely able to see, so I got her a pale blue pashmina, a colour she could see, that went with her eyes, and something wonderfully soft to wear. 'What is it, dear?' she said when I put the parcel in her hands.

'It's a pashmina, Grandy. Finest cashmere.'

She put it down. 'Kind of you, dear, but really not worth opening. Give it to someone else next year.'

She died three weeks later.

'Why do you go on about death so much?' someone snapped at me. 'Why do you fucking think?' I replied, and, chastened, the subject was changed. I think about death all the time, I walk through the valley of its shadow, I deal with the consequences of other people's deaths every day, and with my own grief. This is not surprising, but we recoil from it, because who wants to think about that? I cannot think about anything else since David died, and I have become frightened that everyone else will die too, and when I see my mother and she coughs I think it will be the last time I see her, and when Daisy can't manage to jump up onto the sofa I think Anna the vet is practically at the door with her phials of oblivion.

I went back to the vicarage, to find what looked like a home invasion by a florist. Everything from hand-tied bouquets, to gerberas in a box, to small ornamental trees, were clustered on the doorstep. I took them in, and found vases for as many as I could, put the ornamental tree, an olive from my publisher, in the garden, where, I am pleased to say, it stands in healthful grey-green glory now.

I then went and sat on the sofa and cried. I am rarely moved to tears by things in life, art is another matter, but there is a hygienic purpose to weeping in the first days of grief, a discharge of sorrows that would otherwise disable you, and sometimes weeping came upon me like nausea on a pitching deck, and if I were with people I would hasten away from occupied spaces to find an unoccupied space in which to bawl. They felt too like reverse peristalsis, and would pass in a couple of minutes, and leave me feeling empty, not an unpleasant feeling when you have been full of grief, which sits in you like an indigestible lump of whale meat – not that I have ever eaten whale meat.

Tears voided, I looked at my phone to check emails and Facebook and Twitter; *#ohrichard* was by now trending. Condolences were piling up, a sentence from some, longer from others. Among them I found a fake fundraising page, with a photograph of David, asking for money to pay for his funeral. This broke my silence, and I posted, saying thank you for your condolences, and please ignore the appeal for funeral funds, it's fake.

I read some more, my texts and emails, and found this:

> You will be facing the same fate your David is facing if you're not careful! Scripture is quite clear, and you're unfit for the pastorate! Your David is now a roast on a spit in Hell, you face the same eternity unless you repent! You're as vile as the yank from New Hampshire who divorced his wife to pursue an immoral relationship with a man before being 'consecrated as bishop' by the Episcopal 'Church' of the USA, and then divorcing his 'husband' whom he left his wife and mother of his kids for. You need to leave the pastorate and repent of your immorality! You are not of Christ!

Unusually for a communication of this kind it was signed. It was from another Christian, although a Christian who thought my version of Christianity was not Christianity at all. Two can play at that, and I thought of Jesus saying in the thirteenth chapter of St John's Gospel, 'By this shall all men know that ye are my disciples, if ye have love one to another.'

No love here, not even the pretence of love. I get letters and emails like this from time to time, some signed, most unsigned, from people who do not like me. Some think I fritter my time away making pointless and self-regarding media appearances when I should be consoling the dying and tending the sick. But I do those things in my life as Vicar of Finedon, and they happen away from the cameras and microphones which attend the other half of my existence, as a priest divided between a parish and secular employment. Why people think I only do what they see or hear on television and radio is puzzling, and I suspect not always rational. Some, like my new correspondent, are frank about their dislike of homosexuality, others try to disguise it, and in some it is so intense that there is not even a spark of fellow feeling that I had just lost the love of my life. How could it be the love of my life if it was love that cannot be?

When I first started receiving hostile letters and emails, which came after I started doing *Saturday Live* on Radio Four, they sometimes got under my skin, but in time I ceased to notice them. Or, rather, they lost their power to wound. Now I have in the studio a screen which posts in real time comments on Twitter and by text about the programme and the presenters as it goes out. Most are fine, some are odd, and a few are unpleasant, but I filter them out, of necessity, while we're on air, and afterwards never think of them, or hardly ever. I'm not sure if this is because I have become thick-skinned – I do not want to be thick-skinned particularly – or if familiarity has blunted what once felt like sharpness. This email, exceptionally hateful, did not wound me either, in fact I was more curious than hurt or offended by it, wondering what was going on in the mind of the sender.

I then received a letter, handwritten, which was even stranger. It began:

'Dear Mr Coles, I can't begin to tell you how happy I am to hear of the death of your partner.'

It concluded: 'As long as you continue in your anti-Christ ways your pain will continue, and I will continue to pray

for that, for you and the same for all the others like you.
MERRY CHRISTMAS!!'

I could not quite work out if the sender was annoyed
with me for being a bad Christian or a bad gay, it was rather
confused, and again I was left wondering about the state of
mind of the sender rather than the accusation.

Usually when I receive bizarre hate mail I put it on Facebook, to share the weirdness, and saw no reason not to with
these examples, but perhaps that was a mistake, because it
got a bigger reaction than I had foreseen and was picked
up by the news. I was called and emailed by journalists, all
of whom were sympathetic (I have noticed there is a higher
than normal degree of consideration given by the media to
its own when in crisis), but all wanted to give me 'a chance
to put my side of the story', and I did not want to talk about
it, because I would lose control of it. Posting on social media
myself made me think I was in control of it. I was not. I was
not in control of myself, let alone other people's reactions to
what was happening.

Night fell and I lit a fire, and sat with the dogs on the
sofa watching, or rather looking at, the television. I did not
feel sleepy even though I was exhausted, so I went to the
kitchen to get a whisky to help nudge me along the road
to unconsciousness, and saw, from the corner of my eye, a
bowl on a side table in which David had put his knitting.
It was on two hollow round needles, advanced knitting,
intended as a seamless gansey, so it would not tear on a
boathook used to secure the body of the fisherman wearing
it, his port of origin coded by the pattern on its front. I was
unprepared for it, and the pathos of its incompleteness was
so sudden and intense I began to feel breathless. Eventually
I got my breath back and discovered I was coughing and
felt weirdly febrile so I poured the whisky, a large one, and

took another of David's sleeping pills, a whole one this time, and just made it to bed before unconsciousness made it to me.

I woke, and remembered I was a widow, and a spike of grief met a spike of relief, when I saw I had slept through until seven without interruption, perhaps not surprising after a double whisky and 7.5 mg of Zopiclone, but David was often up in the middle of the night, unwell, and sometimes would forget it was three in the morning and start one of his endless home improvements, or play the violin, or water the garden.

I came downstairs, let the dogs out, made a coffee and a bowl of Alpen – original, full of sugar, comfort food, made by Weetabix – and sat and read my emails. Lots had arrived from people I knew well, and from others I had not heard from in decades. Some were from strangers who had found my email on the parish website, and some were from widows, including two BBC colleagues I had walked alongside in the first days of their widowhoods. I realised, reading condolences, that in my office on the sixth floor of Broadcasting House five of us were now untimely widowed.

But I still felt unqualified, not only unprepared for the loss of my spouse, but not yet properly credentialed without the death certificate. This is part personal – without it I felt I was not entitled to put on widow's weeds and take my rightful place among the shawled and black-fringed cohort to which I now belonged – part bureaucratic, for until you get the death certificate, sadmin's golden ticket, you cannot activate the bereavement algorithms at your banks and HMRC and DVLA and the National Lottery.

Letters were arriving by the sackload. Ozzie, our postman, was having to knock on the door, or leave them in a bundle in the shed, and I discovered in those days following

David's death the utility of the paperknife, which I had always thought as unnecessary as grape scissors or grapefruit spoons, the fussy cutlery kept by my great aunts in their sideboards. There were institutional condolences, or rather condolences passim from former incumbents of Lambeth Palace and Broadcasting House, a kind letter from Lord Carey, former Archbishop of Canterbury, and another from the ruthlessly defenestrated former Director General of the BBC, George Entwistle. There were letters from people I have come to know from social media rather than in the flesh, and in whose company I spend more time than many I know in the flesh. There were lots from strangers, who wrote sometimes a line, sometimes a screed, and there was a continuing abundance of flowers.

I read a pile of letters, and then had to search for suitable vessels for the flowers, which by now had overspilled the sitting room and dining room and study so I had to find spaces for them on windowsills and bookshelves. It was almost a problem.

I took the dogs out, all five, like a cowboy herding miniature cattle, down Harrowden Lane to a path which I knew would be deserted and I could let them off the leads and not have to speak to anyone. I have always loved dog walking, not just for the pleasure of their amusement, but for my own peace of mind. Northamptonshire's wide skies and spreading fields are unlikely to appear in a promotional film for the English Tourist Board, but if you are vulnerable to their peculiar charm it is powerful magic indeed. Walking through that landscape, with dogs or without them, I sometimes feel I am walking where John Clare walked, one of my favourite poets, not footstep in footstep, but my muscles adjusting to the same terrain, the slopes and the turns, my attention caught by the same things, a moorhen on the brook, a wagtail in the lane, a dripping icicle. Not for me the affront of enclosure, but the affront of fields and hedges lost to development, as starter homes advance from Wellingborough, fluttering promotional pennants like a conquering army. I am partly responsible for building them, a board member of the housing association piggybacking on commercial development, because people need places to live.

I found I could both hold and release my grief in the mist and half-light of winter, standing on a path which looked like something from M.R. James, a gate going nowhere, a wonky telegraph pole, and to the west the rattle and shriek of the London train. Another benefit of having dogs is their indifference to your woes and joys. They need what they need – feeding, walking, watering – when they need it, and you have to provide. I remembered my grandmother telling me that, after my grandfather died of a stroke when they were in the middle of building their retirement house, she went into a state of suspension, only relieved when the builder said to her one day, 'Mrs Coles, you have to decide: conservatory or utility?' and she came to herself. She had both, in the end.

I took the dogs back to the vicarage and went to Kettering, where I had arranged to meet Mo and Bryan for lunch before my appointment with the registrar. It is always an adventure with them, and quite often marked by bloodshed and injury. Mo had to be taken to hospital after her seventieth birthday party with a fractured collarbone, and when we first met, on pilgrimage in the Holy Land, our friendship accelerated to intimate terms when she picked up injuries in most of the sacred sites we visited, which David, as a former A&E nurse, took care of. The most dramatic of these was acquired when she gashed a leg getting on the plane on the way home. Her other-worldliness, sustained reasonably safely by Bryan's much more steady grip on this world, is not picturesque or studied but derived from her unflinching sense of the life beyond this life, and for that reason alone she is good to have around when someone dies, not sentimental, not embarrassed. We met at a pizza place just next to the library. It was the first time I had seen them since the deathbed, and we talked about that over margaritas. I told them I had discovered coils of David's knitting the night before – Mo and David were both very keen sewers and knitters – and she said that she would take over, and asked me to gather the bits and bobs so she could finish them for me and for him. We talked, and laughed, so much so that I had to dash to the library, leaving Bryan with the bill, lest I lose my slot.

Every day in lockdown I go out on the bike, and often return up the long hill from Burton Latimer to Finedon, which takes a bit of effort, and a final sprint past a badger, hit by a car and left to die at the side of the road. At first it is fresh, bristly, black and white, poor creature; but in the warm spring soon inflates with post-mortem gases, its legs sticking out comically, and I think of Charles Laughton as Henry Hobson, passed out, flat drunk; and then it deflates, and every day as I cycle past I see the progression of decomposition. It loses its fur, turns brown, and eventually leathery, and, run over from time to time by cars and vans, it is progressively flattened until it starts to look the shape and thickness of an abandoned skateboard. Now only its teeth survive in recognisable form, a semicircle stuck into the surface like a fossil preserved in rock.

*

Kettering library is a Carnegie library, established with funds from the great Scottish-Canadian philanthropist Andrew Carnegie, whose version of giving something back was endowing libraries for the edification of the masses. It has done its work diligently ever since. Next door, and connected, is the Alfred East Gallery, the gift of another eminent Victorian, Sir Alfred East RA, one of the most famous painters of his day, almost forgotten now, an English impressionist who created a sensation when he exhibited work he made in Japan. I have one of his pictures, not of Japan but a moonlit lake across which a ghostly swan glides, a perfectly respectable piece, but rather workaday, made to satisfy a lively market rather than a creative impulse. That came to me via my aunt, grandparents, and great grandparents, one of whom was the son of another of Kettering's eminent Victorians, Owen Robinson. He invented and built the machines for industrialising shoemaking, an enterprise which made my family rich for a hundred years, which is how the painting was acquired. His grandson built a car, the Robinson; the one remaining, built for a local doctor with a fold-down operating table on the back for whipping out appendixes, is permanently parked in Kettering's museum, next to the gallery. This is the town's Heritage Quarter, or Heritage Eighth perhaps, a seat of learning, art, invention, and the officers of the Crown.

Mine was a young man, a deputy registrar, who collected me from a chair outside his office and invited me to sit not across his desk, but next to it, like a GP's surgery. He offered me professional condolences, for which I thanked him, and then he explained what I had to do, what he had to do, how much it would cost, and invited me to ask any questions I might have. I gave him my forms and he checked them, and I noted that he had a mug bearing a scarlet liver bird, the blazon of Liverpool Football Club, so the question I asked him was what he made of Jürgen Klopp rather than anything to do with the process of registering David's death. I quite liked having a cue to take me somewhere other than David's death, and afterwards I wondered if others did the same, tear-blurred eyes alighting on an artfully placed object.

I do not know if his mug was artfully placed, but something else definitely was, a yellow sign, at eye level, which advised, in bold black print, that anyone giving false information or making a false declaration to the registrar risks prosecution for perjury. I noticed it not only for its conspicuousness, but because an identical sign had been carefully placed in the office of a different registrar where I had applied for the civil partnership David and I entered into nine years earlier. It struck me that our officially recognised relationship was bookended by these two signs, admonition from officialdom rather than celebration and lament. I knew a little about that because David and I were both registrars too, ex officio as licensed clerics of the Church of England, permitted and required to keep a Register of Marriages in our parishes. A wedding is perhaps the most familiar liturgy of the Church of England, but it is also one of the weirdest, for in it the sacred and the secular collide rather than harmonise, and a woman in a big white dress and a man in a tailcoat sign legal documents between the nuptial blessing and Mendelssohn's Wedding March. There is a structural tension between clerical and civil registrars, a legal boundary between their authority and ours, which is why you cannot officially have God at a civil ceremony, although you may believe, as I do, that God is already there whether the law likes it or not. I remember once having to work out where the boundary lay when friends asked me for a blessing at their civil ceremony which I attended as a guest. The registrar said that when he closed the book he considered his duties discharged. He closed it, with an empathetic flourish, and I raised my hand in a gesture of blessing, and then we all went for lunch at a country house hotel.

It was a more complicated matter for me and David because the Church, which issued our licences to officiate, does not recognise the holiness of our relationship, so there are emphatically no official blessings for us, and we have to make do with unofficial blessings, which fortunately are no less puissant.

When I conduct a marriage or a funeral there is the matter of money, for despite the transcendent character of these ceremonies, bills need to be raised and paid. At a wedding the parish clerk normally takes care of that, and at a funeral the funeral directors discreetly pass the officiating minister a brown envelope, once with cash inside, now cheques. Registering a death also attracts a fee, a cost for the certificate itself – it was £4 but had recently been increased, swingeingly, to £11, which the registrar seemed quite embarrassed about. I wondered how many I would need and he explained that was up to me, but I would need to send a copy, or if I were lucky scan a copy, to various interested bodies, who would return it, but it would be sensible to invest in more than one. I decided on four in the end, and paid my £44, and he printed them off, signed them, and handed them to me. There it was, in the same typeface, on the same paper, and bearing the same crest, as our certificate of civil partnership. David was now officially dead as far as the United Kingdom of Great Britain and Northern Ireland was concerned. The document was to be entered into the record, there for posterity to consult, for statistics to be calculated. I thought of how much David liked certificates, this man of many accomplishments, who had framed and hanging in his study not only his bishops' licences but his qualifications in nursing, in applied design, even one in barbering.

Sadmin, the bureaucracy of bereavement, is useful. Partly this is because it is something that simply must be done, partly because every time you tidy something up in chaotic circumstances an angel sings in tune, but also because it tells you with clarity what you need to know – that your 'loved one' has really gone.

It also told me something else, baldly, in black type.

The cause of David's death was three-tiered.

GI bleed.

Spontaneous perforation of the oesophagus.

Chronic decompensated alcoholic liver disease.

David's illness was alcohol addiction. He was an alcoholic, although I do not like to describe a person in all his complexity in so simplistic a way. It is a therapeutic handle, useful for the person recovering from addiction, who needs to grasp it first; but David had not recovered from it, he had died because of it, and I do not want him to be reduced to a word both too narrow to tell you what you need to know about him, and too narrowing of sympathetic engagement for those on the outside of the exacting and tragic and moving and heroic and impossible love that happens between addicts and their dependants.

He had always liked to drink, he liked the pub, and a glass of wine, and whisky nightcap. Sometimes he would binge, go out with a drinking friend and come home drunk and fall asleep, unrousably, in an armchair. I did not give this much thought, because hard drinking is not unusual among gay men or medics or High Church clergy, and David was all three. Gay men find their feet in clubs and pubs, where alcohol acts as a solvent of anxiety, among other things. The worst of life is the daily diet of nurses in A&E, which incentivises drowning not only their own sorrows but the sorrows of everyone else too. I was cellarer at my theological college, a position which required me to provide alcohol for my fellow students, and it was not the odd bottle of dry sherry that filled my shopping bags when I returned from the bargain off-licences of industrial West Yorkshire, but gin, cheap gin, with slightly sinister and obscure labels, and drinking it to excess was so much part of clerical life I came to call it Father's Ruin.

Perhaps this is also something to do with a need to palliate pain, in which gay men, nurses, and clergy are expert? There was something of self-medication in David's drinking. When he was stressed, or anxious, or unsure of himself, drink was effective, in the short term at any rate, accessible, and socially acceptable. At least, it was until it became uncontrollable.

I think it was not only to self-medicate that David drank. Sometimes he drank vocationally, with a curiosity, and commitment, and dedication. I remember once, on holiday in Scotland, we had whiskies from local distilleries to try. On the last night, after I went to bed, David decided to finish them off, and when I woke I found him unconscious in the sitting room, kneeling on the floor in a peculiar attitude of obeisance, surrounded by now empty bottles of Springbank and Glen Scotia. When I roused him he said he had been conducting an experiment, and then slept all the way home.

David had a breakdown not long after we arrived at Finedon. I had not seen it coming. I thought he was content. We had just become civil partners, he was serving as a non-stipendiary curate in the neighbouring parish, and working as an occupational health adviser at Weetabix, down the road. I used to see him off to work in the morning, in his suit, and hair net and beard snood, I remember thinking how happy he looked.

He was not happy. Something went wrong, he took on too much, I was away too often, he was lonely, I was too absorbed by my things to notice.

That was when he started to drink uncontrollably. His

personality changed when he was drunk, the alcohol charging and releasing dark impulses that made him at first difficult, and then obnoxious. Our social life became embarrassing, then impossible. He lost his job. He lost his licence from the bishop, which curtailed his ministry, to the regret of many who had begun to enjoy it, and he nearly lost me, because I could not at first stop being angry with him for inflicting this damage on himself and on me and on our happiness.

At its worst I would come home, and sit in my car on the drive, wondering what awaited inside. I had to nerve myself to go in, and find him passed out on the floor, surrounded by broken glass, the dogs desperate to be fed and watered and let out.

And then, at its worst, after an episode of such appalling behaviour the police were involved, and I started to enquire discreetly about a place to rent nearby so I could at least get some sleep at night, I stopped being angry with him.

I think this happened, first, because I started attending Al Anon, the offshoot of Alcoholics Anonymous for the benefit of those who love members of the original organisation, and there I learned from others further down the path; second, because David, in a conversation with someone, said he was scared I would leave him, and the person burst out laughing and said, 'If he was going to leave you he would have gone by now.' And third, the grace of God, which comes when you really need it.

I stopped being angry with him because I loved him, and he did not need me to make him feel any worse than he was already feeling.

He stopped getting drunk, drunk to the point of oblivion, but I realised that he was still drinking and would not stop drinking. The pattern changed, he would have a 'Coke' always to hand, which was not just Coke, although we never alluded to that. And when I checked the empties in the recycling bin I realised he was getting through almost as much as he ever had, only in smaller, better-regulated doses.

David could not manage without drink, I tried everything I could think of to get him off it, but going without was sometimes more terrible than his worst drunkenness, and he could not give it up. Although, made manageable, so much of him that was lovable and sweet was salvaged, the damage it had wrought on his liver, and pancreas, and heart, and brain was terrible. Drunkenness was replaced by debilitating physical dysfunction, which in some ways was as hard to bear as the drunkenness, and made me frustrated and angry again.

One of my fears is having to speak reason to someone without reason. When David was drunk there was no point, and I did not try, but harder than drunkenness was denial, and when, because of necessity, I had to deal with a reality he would not deal with, because it would involve facing the reality of his drinking, I could explode with a temper I did not know I had. One of the worst explosions was the last explosion, a week before he was taken ill, when I discovered that he was about to take out a lease on a shop and a cafe, and was going to start a craft centre, and had started ordering equipment and crockery and a potter's wheel and a new kiln, with money we could not spare, for a project he could not possibly undertake because he was too ill. To David, I realise now, it was a last defence against the death he sensed was coming, so when I confronted him about it he had only resistance, and would not hear, could not hear, reason. And because of that, and because I too must have understood on some level that he was on the edge of the abyss, and it frightened me, I lost my temper and shouted at him, I screamed at him.

When this had happened in the past, he would mock me and say, sarcastically, 'Britain's best-loved vicar?' which would make me laugh and, anger neutralised, we could move on. But this time he retreated from me into the kitchen, and then doubled over in pain and started gulping for air. I thought he was being melodramatic. But he was not being melodramatic. My anger produced a physical reaction in him, a recoil, not only him from me, but within his body, and he started to retch and heave. I forgot my anger when I realised his pain, which was so much greater, and we calmed down. I am ashamed of having lost my temper, and feel guilty that my verbal violence caused him physical injury. I think, I fear, it contributed to his death.

One of the hardest wishes since his death is that I had not lost my temper with him but had been tender and loving, for he loved nothing more; and when I was not tender and loving it hurt him so much.

'Won't you be lonely?' someone says when I say after the funeral that I am going to Wales for a week. Yes, I think, but I want to be lonely, I want to spend some time on my own far from home, with the dogs, and a rented bike to struggle up hills and coast down them, even the steepest now made accessible by the wonderful invention of electric pedal assist. I found a cottage to rent at the edge of the Brecon Beacons, up a hill, no neighbours, with a view across the valley.

I am not completely alone. One of my teammates on the victorious University Challenge *squad I captained just before David fell ill lives nearby. We had met only once, recording the programme, but we just liked each other straight away, more on the axis of difference than similarity. Tim is a wildlife photographer and to describe him as outdoorsy would be to undersell his commitment to raw adventure. I think I sensed this, and knew that as a Poor Tom, lost on a blasted heath, Tim might be a useful travelling companion. I call, and he comes by one morning to pick me and the dogs up in a jeep, the back of which looks like it is designed to accommodate wolfhounds rather than tiny dachshunds. My cottage is right on the edge of the high country, so we drive up along twisting roads between grey thorny hedges that get narrower and rougher, intersected occasionally by a line of telegraph poles linking the distant farms, so remote you wonder if in some they still think there is a war on. We park next to a hill, not too steep, invitingly green, and in the distance at the top a circlet of trees. 'That's where we're going,' says Tim.*

We set off, the dogs looking suspiciously at distant sheep, but they stick with us, and we walk and splash and push our way through gorse and puddles. The distant circle of trees is more distant than I thought; and suddenly a damson-dark ridge of clouds appears behind us, pushing a mighty wind, and suddenly it begins to hail. Not just hail, it is like being caught in a gun battle in an Arctic storm and I assume we will dive for cover or head back, but Tim keeps on going as if he has not even noticed the life-threatening weather that encircles us. The dogs, bedraggled, uncertain, are doing their best to keep up and I picture the newspaper headline: Britain's Best-Loved Vicar Dead of Exposure.

And then as quickly as it descended, the storm lifts, as we arrived at the top, where a low-walled enclosure provides some cover from the petering rain. The sun comes out and spreads light across the huge landscape in front of us and sparkles where it strikes the river, far below, which threads with quicksilver the patchwork of fields and hedges stretching from Wales to England. It is better than anything words could do, and we drink hot coffee from a flask while looking at the splendour and the drama of the view, and then we talk with an intimacy and trust that comes from nowhere and, once offered and accepted, means friendship.

THE MADNESS OF GRIEF

*

I took a copy of the death certificate with me to my next appointment with the funeral directors. I went to their office, where I had never been before, because in spite of working with them all the time it has always been in the field, literally for some burials. Like many funeral directors, the traditional kind not yet bought up by the big corporates, they occupy a yard, a sort of stockade, with an office section, a storage section, a processing section, and a garage. Many began as joiners, coffin-making one of their daily duties, but in time the smart joiners realised that there was more money to be made in that part of their business than any other and over a generation or two devoted themselves entirely to it, undertaking (hence the name) all the funeral arrangements, as well as making the coffins.

They don't make coffins any more. They come from a catalogue which Michael, the back office brother, had on a shelf behind his desk. It was the first time we had met face to face, although we had spoken almost every week for ten years. I also met the people in the front office, who answer the phone, disembodied voices suddenly made flesh. Everyone was kind and sympathetic.

It is an odd feeling for a cleric to be a mourner rather than an officiant. As officiants we relate to funeral directors as fellow professionals, and the work being the work of death, a black-tinged banter is normal. Stories of funerals gone wrong, or the spectacularly unusual, fill the offstage moments, but all that goes when your role switches. I was prepared for this because I had buried my father with another firm in the town nearby, where my parents lived, and the director and the bearers, normally offstage, were on stage, solemn and formal.

There was another shift. Michael gave me his condolences

and then said that their father, old Mr Abbott, from whom they had taken over the business, had just died and that they too were mourning. I gave him my condolences, priest rather than mourner at that moment, and then we readjusted back to the business in hand.

I handed over the documents he needed – always forms to exchange in a church by law established – and we looked at the diary. Dying at Christmas, which is not unusual, is very inconvenient, because of the holidays, which would fall between David's death and his funeral, and the seasonal rush on caterers and florists for Christmas and New Year might leave the cupboard and the back room bare when we needed them. Also Christmas fell midweek, which meant people were likely not to go back to work before New Year. We provisionally chose the third of January, the nearest convenient date, soon enough to be timely, but long enough for a return to work for those returning, and a Friday so if people were coming from far away they would have a weekend following. It would need to be confirmed with gravediggers, Grafton Underwood church, the cricket club for the knees-up afterwards, the caterers.

I had already thought about someone to officiate. I knew I did not want to do it because I would want to mourn, not work, so I asked Martyn Percy, the Dean of Christ Church and David's former principal at theological college, to officiate at the funeral, and my curate Jane, approaching her first Christmas as a priest, to officiate at the burial.

It was the little things rather than the big things that made me feel suddenly overwhelmed. The notification in the paper, the flowers, the car parking. Michael, practised in such things, saw it, and reminded me that their job was to undertake, and I need not worry.

I did need to make some decisions. The coffin, for example.

Down came the catalogue, and I flicked through, wishing David were there to advise me because he had such a good eye for these things and would take care to get whatever he appeared in just right. I made the selection like someone on a first date in a restaurant, choosing wine not from the bottom of the list nor the top, but midrange. There I found a line named after cathedral cities and eventually chose a Norwich. David had been ordained in its cathedral and it seemed as near to fitting as I would ever get, that he should go into eternity embraced by the see in which he was ontologically, eternally, altered.

The funeral service itself I was more confident about, funerals are what I do; but priest funerals, if done traditionally, differ. Priests are buried in vestments, holding a chalice and paten, tools of our trade, and the wrong way round, with the feet at the headstone, according to a rather picturesque clerical tradition that we will rise in the general resurrection to face the people as we did in life. I am nothing like as punctilious in these matters as I used to be, and David was never punctilious about them, but I did want David's dignity as a priest to be observed. So he would be buried in vestments, the wrong way round, in the grave reserved for us in the churchyard at Grafton Underwood, on the north side near the chancel, where priests who had served there since the thirteenth century, known and unknown, were also buried.

The High Church custom is also to have a Requiem Mass, with Holy Communion, for a funeral, but David would not have wanted that, and it would have set a high hurdle for many of the people coming who were not Christians, so we decided to have the standard funeral service from the Church of England's provision. Another tradition we would follow was receiving the coffin into church on the evening before, where it would lie, under a pall – a giant holy bedspread made for this purpose – through the night.

This I would officiate at, and it would be only for David's family and for his closest friends, because at a big funeral intimacy is often lost to ceremony, and this would give us a chance to be alone with him. At my last parish we did the funeral for Alexander McQueen, the fashion designer, one of the few funerals I have known where there was an issue with paparazzi. It was so big, so glamorous, so A list, that his family looked slightly on the edge of it rather than at the centre, and I wished we had invited them to church the night before so they could have had some time with him to themselves. Instead he lay alone after Evening Prayer, save the company of a former SAS security guard hired by Gucci, whom we locked in with him.

David's funeral would be nothing like that, but Michael said he thought there would be a lot of 'interest', and did I want to view the body? I did not, and did not want anyone else to – David hated his emaciated appearance in the last weeks of his life – but perhaps it would be important to other people? Michael gently pointed out that there was a lot of media interest and his staff might not always be able to tell the difference between a family member and a journalist. It had not occurred to me, until then, that intrusion of this kind might be a problem. I decided against a viewing.

I drove home, but was consumed by the thought of people wanting to view his body, and that brought another wave of grief. Driving while grief-stricken is not to be recommended. This is not because you weave across the road like a drunk or texting driver, but because everything is on autopilot – I would turn into the vicarage drive and realise I could not remember a single thing about how I had got there – and I wonder now if I was entirely safe. I thought I was, but at the time I thought I was functioning as normal, and I know now I was not.

When I got back I heard from a churchwarden that she, and the parish clerk, and anyone else whose name and number was on the website, had been called by journalists, and one or two had been knocking on doors and asking questions about David around the parish. It was not the first time journalists had been interested in me, although for less catastrophic reasons till now, and the parish is almost too careful not to say anything to them when they call. I really did not want to have to deal with this. The last thing I needed, with my life out of control, was another uncontrollable element, and intrusive attention. When someone dies everyone wants to know why they died. Most are tactful and will neither ask nor seek clues, but some are direct and some subtle. I did not want every tier of David's cause of death to be known, I did not want them to talk about his drinking, nor did I want his parents to have to deal with that, because I did not want him in all his glory to be debased by 'tragic drunk' clichés. And I most definitely did not want Irene and Vinnie and David's family, who I would have to call to give due warning, to have to deal with this.

I was thinking about that when there was a ring on the doorbell and I answered it with the trepidation I usually feel for the 3 a.m. summons by someone who is mentally unwell, or a someone with a bag of dusters I do not want, and a tale to tell I've heard before.

It was Jane, my curate.

She came in, to the delight of the dogs, who had taken to her in the eighteen months she had been with us, a very important test of vocation in this vicarage. Jane's vocation was late, like mine, and she had, and maintains, a parallel and distinguished career in charity fundraising before she put on her collar. The first time you see an ordinand in the collar is telling, for you scrutinise them to see if it looks right. It did look right on Jane, harmonising with her red hair, freckles, no-nonsense manner, and searching and intelligent look.

We had a drink, and she asked me how I was and what I wanted to do. Talking about the rota made me feel suddenly a little self-conscious in my slippers and scamper pants, which is what David and I called 'loungewear' because I cannot bear the word 'lounge', and I said something ridiculous about not being properly dressed, and Jane snorted and said she preferred me in scampers to clericals. There is, in theory, a proper distance between training incumbent and curate, necessary for the preservation of authority, but I have never found this a theory that holds – I became friends with both my incumbents when I was a curate – and I had immediately got on with Jane too, despite being different in churchman-ship, as it is called. Not a problem for me, and I have valued being made to think about why I do things my way when there is another way, but the dynamic of a boss in grief, how-ever, is different, and I wondered if it might be awkward for her. It was not, and I did not hesitate to ask her to co-officiate with Martyn at David's funeral, and preside at the burial at Grafton Underwood which would follow immediately after. She agreed, and I felt a little victory for having decided and secured something, a foothold on the north face of Mount Grief, and one step of ascent to whatever lay at the top.

After Jane went, I got on the WhatsApp group I had set up for David's family to update them on the arrangements, and to warn them that there may be interest from journalists, and they might want to think about what they wanted to say if asked to say something. 'I don't want to say anything,' said Irene, 'and no one in the family will say anything either.' I talked also to Mark about giving the tribute at the funeral, which he said he would be pleased to do.

I ate something. I had a bath. I watched television and then at about ten there was another ring on the doorbell, and another reason to feel mild apprehension. I could see through the coloured glass the screamingly yellow blousons of police officers. What fresh hell is this? I thought, and opened the door to an inspector and a sergeant.

They had come because of the hostile letters and emails I had received. These had generated some interest on social media and in the news, which I had not been following, so I was surprised to see them; surprised not only because I was not expecting them, but because I did not consider them so offensive as to merit police attention. I invited them in, and installed them on the Sofa of Tears in my study, so called for on it people in distress frequently weep, and made tea. For the second time that night I felt improperly dressed, in scampers and slippers while they, bristling with clip-on tech and weaponry, produced a clipboard and some forms. No weeping tonight, I thought. The sergeant produced a hand-held gadget, just out, which allowed them to input information across a number of digital platforms, whatever that means. I wondered for a moment if she might have absentmindedly deholstered her taser instead and I was about to be accidentally shot.

I said I appreciated their interest but it wasn't my intention to make a complaint, a polite way of saying 'haven't you got anything better to do?' I suppose. The inspector said that he thought it unwise to ignore a hate crime for at least two reasons: first, that it might escalate if not checked; and second, that it might not bother me, but the authors might write to others who would be bothered by it. I do not like the expression hate crime because it seems to me too broad if it gives equal billing to unpleasant letters and actual acts of violence, but again he said the two are not unrelated, and better to tackle it sooner rather than later.

That seemed to me to make sense. And while I say I was unaffected by hostile attention, actually I think I was – not so much by the crazy stuff, although every blow lands, but more by cruel remarks from people who should know better. The worst of these came from another Anglican priest, who took the trouble to say that while it was regrettable that David had died it in no way affected his firm belief that we were both unfit to be public representatives of the Christian faith. Someone writing crazy stuff in a mental maelstrom is much easier to forgive than someone calmly thinking about it and sending something so heartless, so indifferent to the suffering of the newly bereaved.

The inspector asked me if he could see the letter, which I found but handled more casually than he did, which made him slightly wince. He produced an evidence bag and sealed it in that, and asked me if I had the envelope too, but I had thrown it away. I gave a statement, which he took down, and said he would send to me for approval before it was entered into the eternity of digital storage. There was some form-filling, some evidentially necessary caveats pronounced, and then his sergeant tried to get the new gadget to work to input some information, but it did not work, and I saw in their professional life what was so familiar from mine, and so many others, the disempowering pantomime of pretending you know what you are doing with the new technology when actually you do not. In the end they fixed it but by then it was past eleven o'clock and I began to droop.

They made to leave, but the sergeant then said, 'He's got something to show you.'

'What's that?'

The inspector looked embarrassed. 'It's nothing . . .'

'Go on,' she said, '*show him.*'

'Yes, show me,' I said.

He produced his phone.

'It's the alarm,' the sergeant said. 'Play it!'

He did. It was one of my own records. 'I wake up to that every morning,' he said.

'There are no words . . .' There are only words, but they are inadequate, and when people ask me how I am, and want to know, I find it harder and harder to answer. I say, 'I am standing up and facing forward,' which is true enough and socially palatable, but it is not always true to say that motion follows. Sometimes I am stuck, and a day goes by when I think of nothing but something I said, or did, which I wish were different. It induces a sort of paralysis.

To some I say, 'It sucks,' because it is true, but there is faint comedy in it, coming from a vicar and a widow, and it neutralises my anxiety that it will provoke their anxiety.

To a few I say how I feel; to David's mum, to my family, to the friends whom I think will not be unnerved or bored.

'There are no words . . .' I stand on my balcony, midships, as evening falls and watch a big swell loom, darker than the surrounding waters, distant, then under us, lifting the whole ship in such an unexpected way that your perception, and your body, take a second to catch up.

O Key of David

I woke the next day and tried to say Morning Prayer. The run-up to Christmas is heralded by the Great O Antiphons, a set of short introductory prayers for every day in the week preceding. The Great Os, as they are known, date from at least the fifth century, and were sung in the Benedictine monasteries of France when the abbot would give a present to each of the monks as the series progressed. Eventually their use spread throughout the Church, although in England, being England, we did them a little differently from everyone else. Some say the seven titles form an acrostic, EROCRAS, the Latin for 'tomorrow I will be'. They acclaim the coming of Jesus Christ on the seven days using seven titles derived from the Jewish prophecies of the Old Testament.

The Great O Antiphon for that morning is 'Clavis David', Key of David. I flinched to say the name. Isaiah in the Old Testament prophesied that the Messiah will bear 'on his shoulder the key of the house of David; he shall open, and no one shall shut; he shall shut, and no one shall open' and that he will 'bring out the prisoners from the prison, and them that sit in darkness out of the prison house'. This image is recalled in the Icon of the Resurrection, when we see Jesus trampling down the gates of hell and rescuing from its pit Adam and Eve, of the old covenant, who shake off their locks and chains as they enter the new. I could not handle the words, but I could look at the icon. I have a copy of the version in the church at my old theological college, and I thought again of the ominous pointing Paddington outside David's hospital room. Why did that come into my mind? I think in moments of intense disturbance our attention is held not by words but by figures, not fleshed-out characters, but symbols perhaps, the better able to serve as signposts in the unfamiliar and frightening world of bereavement.

Christ trampling the gates of hell I could contemplate, Paddington, his paw raised like Death's arm in *The Seventh Seal*, I could contemplate. Christmas coming, heralded by the Key of David and Santa Claus, I could not, and I felt that falling sensation again at the thought. What would I do?

Before Christmas I went to stay with Lorna, my former manager, and friend of forty years. She had also invited a friend of equal duration, Kevin, whom I had first met in the early eighties when we were both living in London around what sociologists now call the Alternative Gay Scene. Kevin was now retired, living half in the Borough, half in São Paolo, and in the middle of arranging his marriage to his Brazilian partner. I could not think of two people I would rather see in a place I would sooner visit than them, at Lorna's house. It would be my first excursion from home since David's death, my first opportunity to see friends whom I had known all my adult life, and with whom I had gone through its pitch and toss. For that reason I was apprehensive, because I thought seeing them might cause a pit explosion and ignite all manner of volatile things, and bring to the surface dark materials, and that was an overwhelming thought. But it had to be done, that staging-post passed, and I knew also what you only know when you have done decades of friendship with someone: that they have seen the best and the worst of you, and are still standing.

I could not take the dogs. Not only because you cannot take five dogs visiting anywhere, really, but because Lorna has cats who we thought would make bad hosts. I did not want to leave them, because they had been left enough, and because the change of routine and the absence of David must affect them, and I supposed some steadiness would be the desirable day, but I was not steady, so I dropped them with friends, and set off for Sussex but via Oxford, where I was having lunch with Martyn at Christ Church to discuss the funeral.

I remember nothing about the journey there save a stop for petrol near Towcester, when I drove carelessly into the path of a juggernaut, who had to jam his brakes on, and was put out by that, and expressed himself with eloquent gestures. I felt a surge of rage and wanted to scream at him I HAVE JUST LOST THE LOVE OF MY LIFE, CAN'T YOU TELL?

Could anyone tell? I felt like a leper in those first days of grief, wrapped in my misfortune, sounding like a broken bell, and contagious with bad luck, so I imagined people kept their distance from me. Perhaps, because the news of David's death, and the weird correspondence, had spread, they were keeping their distance, from respect for my feelings or because of their own awkwardness?

Oxford is, with Cambridge, my least favourite place to attempt to park in the world, its regulations so malevolently, donnishly impossible I normally use the Park and Ride, which works out cheaper than the fine for breaking one of the invisible rules which pertain in the city centre; but Martyn had offered me a parking space at Christ Church and given directions to get there, which I got wrong, and ended up scraping along a street narrow even by medieval standards before I found the back gate, where a helpful man in an unlikely costume admitted me to its spreading, gravelled acres.

I parked and he directed me to the Dean's House, a door in a quad with a bell that you heard distantly ring about five seconds after you pressed it, or pulled it, I don't remember which. Someone came to the door and let me in and led me through a hall to Martyn's study, which is about the size of Leicester Cathedral. The Dean of Christ Church is rather slight, with a neat beard, greying rapidly, and not at all like the voluminous notables who have preceded him in that double role, first as a cathedral dean, with responsibility for running a great ecclesiastical establishment, notoriously tricky, and in the university as Dean of College too, even trickier, given that he is required, through personality, compromise, and silkiness, to get fractious, independently minded corporate bodies to play nicely. It would be hard to think of anywhere more challenging than Christ Church at that time, and Martyn, who was still fighting a bitter Oxford battle ruthless even by the standards of a Senior Common Room, gave me his condolences with the rueful expression of another who was going through the mill.

'How are you?' 'Not great.' 'How are you?' 'Not great.'

He gave me a tour which led, at the end, through French windows to the garden. It looked familiar. Had I been there before? I don't think I had, but I recognised it when Martyn reminded me that it had been home to Alice Liddell, daughter of a Victorian dean, who in 1865 so captivated the college's assistant librarian, Charles Dodgson, that he wrote for her, about her, *Alice in Wonderland*. That is what I recognised; the tree in which the Cheshire Cat appeared, the door to the cathedral gardens, locked to her as a child, beyond which

96

such wonders awaited. I had seen them in a documentary, or an adaptation, on television, but seeing them in reality made me stumble.

There is something about fantasy worlds that is unhelpful when you are trying to accept a hard lesson in the real world. The prospect of a place beyond this place where every terrible deficit is restored is bitter to behold. You might think this ironic, considering my vocation, and location, but the hope of eternity in Christ is not, I have found, a source of comfort or solace, or not much. It is much more challenge than comfort, because it requires us to live so differently here in anticipation of what awaits, without shirking what all those who would live faithfully in Christ must do: to take up the cross.

There is a theological neatness and a flattering heroism in taking up the cross, if we are not careful. It can be insulting to those who endure non-theoretical suffering, and watching David, whose sufferings were gruelling and cruel, had caused me enough suffering to flinch if I suspected someone was about to help with that.

No danger of any of that nonsense from Martyn. We talked practicalities over plates of sandwiches, served by his PA, about the shape of the service – regular funeral rather than Requiem Mass, coffin in on the eve, about Jane taking care of the burial after the funeral, about Mark giving the eulogy. Martyn asked me to make some notes for him, the salient points of David's life, for reference when he wrote what he was going to say.

I had already decided readings and music and hymns, two mainstream, one a little niche. We would begin with 'Dear Lord and Father of Mankind', partly because everyone knows it; partly because we sang it once on a ship in the middle of the Sea of Galilee and it made David weep;

and partly because he had such a keen sense of our need for forgiveness. We would go out to 'Guide Me O Thou Great Redeemer' to the tune 'Cwm Rhondda', because it is a belter that everyone knows, and it sends us out as he is sent out, Jordan bound, and for what lies beyond the Jordan. And in the middle we would have 'How Shall I Sing That Majesty?' to the tune 'Coe Fen', which for theological college alumni of our vintage and churchmanship is like 'The Great Escape' for England football fans. I knew what music we would come in to as well: Vaughan Williams' organ prelude on the Welsh hymn tune 'Rhosymedre'.

For the readings, I knew I wanted one of my favourite passages from the New Testament, from the letter to the Ephesians:

> Although I am the very least of all the saints, this grace was given to me to bring to the Gentiles the news of the boundless riches of Christ, and to make everyone see what is the plan of the mystery hidden for ages in God who created all things; so that through the church the wisdom of God in its rich variety might now be made known . . . I pray that you may have the power to comprehend, with all the saints, what is the breadth and length and height and depth, and to know the love of Christ that surpasses knowledge, so that you may be filled with all the fullness of God.

To read it I asked the theologian Lucy Dallas, a friend of ours, who was at college with David.

And I also wanted the story of 'The Princess and the Pea' from the tales of Hans Christian Andersen. David had been so notoriously fastidious about bedlinen and cushions and decor generally that I once said, irritated, that he made the princess in the story look like Calamity Jane. To read it, I asked another friend, Kate Bottley, 'media vicar' like me.

From Finedon, I asked our friend Jonathan Reynolds, who was David's singing teacher, to sing 'Climb Ev'ry Mountain' from *The Sound of Music*, one of David's favourite films, which we had to watch in our pyjamas on the evening of Christmas Day, an observance kept as zealously as Midnight Mass the night before.

Martyn's wife Emma appeared and gave me her condolences and I gave her my commiserations for their travails too, and thought how miserable it must be to live among one's enemies in the daily round of cathedral worship and college life. Imagine meeting on the stairs people who wish and seek your ruin? Or having to exchange the peace with them at the Eucharist? I looked out of the window at the Alice door in the garden wall and understood why a don might write about the magical world beyond, but denied.

Martyn saw me to my car, and I nodded at the extravagantly costumed gatekeeper who let me out, and I left Oxford behind me, triggering numberplate recognition technologies as I motored out of the city by another unauthorised route.

I thought of calling in at Cuddesdon, David's old theological college. He transferred there after doing a year at St Stephen's House, also in Oxford, but in the Victorian sprawl of the Cowley Road rather than green fields, where Martyn had been principal. We were three years into our relationship when he went there, and I was curate at St Paul's Knightsbridge, so I would take the bus from Hyde Park to Oxford on my day off, and vice versa on his. I remembered once him coming to meet me off the bus in the Cowley Road with a horribly bruised face. What had happened? Late at night, in a dark street, he had seen a woman being attacked and got into a fight with her assailant. Why had he not told me? He had not thought to, because getting punched held no fears for him after years of A&E, and although he did not look like the incarnation of muscular Christianity, he was fearless in a fight.

Cuddesdon is a village set at a suitable distance from the dreaming spires and toxic corridors of the city and the college there has been to the Church of England what Sandhurst is to the British Army. Countless bishops have trained in it since the Bishop of Oxford, Soapy Sam Wilberforce, opened a training college in the grounds of his episcopal palace in 1853. The saintly bishops Edward King and Charles Gore had taught there, Robert Runcie, the last Archbishop of Canterbury but three, had been principal, as had one of my teachers at King's College London, Leslie Houlden, and Archbishop Michael Ramsey, and the Bishop of Norwich, who was David's sponsoring bishop, and the then Bishop of London, my bishop at that time, were all alumni.

David had finished his ordination training there, after the spikier Anglo-Catholic establishment off the Cowley Road, in both places keeping Daisy, our double dappled long-haired miniature dachshund, in contravention of the rules. Daisy lived in his room, when she wasn't running into other ordinands' rooms if they left their doors open, and under his cassock, where he stowed her for services in chapel, once interrupting matins with a startled bark when they both awoke after a long setting of the Te Deum.

A surge of grief hit me, and I had to stop. I decided not to revisit Cuddesdon, not today, because the thought of him there, and Daisy with him, was too much.

David and I met on 1 July 2007, the day of the smoking ban, an irony considering his unfailing devotion to that habit. It was in a church in Norwich, St John's Timberhill, high and spiky, and I remember someone making a timely joke about its overworked thurible producing more fumes than a pub in midwinter. I was there to preach at my friend Christopher's First Mass, his first go presiding at the Eucharist after ordination to the priesthood. I noticed a young and handsome man in the congregation, particularly noticeable because such places are not over busy accommodating that demographic.

At the Communion I assisted with the distribution, and he appeared in my queue, which required him to move from one side of the church to the other. He always denied this, but I think he did. After the service I was in the vestry signing the book when he appeared and introduced himself: 'I'm David. I'm on the PCC.' We talked for a bit, just pleasantries, and then I said, in a moment of inspiration, 'Have you got a fag?'

We stood outside, on a blazingly hot day, me sweating in a cassock, he in his Sunday best. He was beautifully dressed, always well turned out, the antithesis to my frumpy dishevelment. And handsome, dark-haired, dark-eyed, fifteen years younger, and totally not my type. He gave me his last Marlboro Light. I did not know it at the time, but to him that was like giving a stranger his last pint of blood. We went to Tesco to buy some more and he told me about his life. He was recently returned from South Africa where he had been working as a nurse in a clinic in a township on the edge of the city, but was now running the occupational health at Anglian. 'Anglian Windows?' I said. 'Anglian Home Improvements,' he replied. He said he was a lifelong churchgoer and was now interested in exploring his vocation and could he come and see me to discuss it? I said of course. I was living in Boston in Lincolnshire at the time, my first parish as curate, on the other side of the Wash from Norfolk, but not that far away.

The following Sunday he turned up at my house, an odd

but likeable place on the river Witham, built by a boatbuilder, and you could tell because it had a slightly maritime feel to it, all pitch pine and tongue and groove. I gave him lunch, which he later told me was disgusting, and then we talked shop. We talked all afternoon. I was very proper, very professional. The clock struck half past five, and it was time for me to go to Evensong. He said, can I come and see you again? I said, yes, let's make an appointment for a month or six weeks and see where you've got to. I said goodbye, shook his hand, and walked to church thinking, what a nice young man. Then my phone buzzed in my pocket.

It was a text from David.

Don't you get it?

And that was that.

I continued south, towards Lorna and Kevin. I wanted to be with them not only for the security that your oldest and closest friends provide, but because my friendship with them precedes, and is independent of, David. I think now I was trying to face forwards, because I had to, I could not look backwards, because at that moment it made my loss overwhelming. So I wanted to look to the future, which would have Kevin and Lorna in it, when David would be a memory, in the past. You do what you have to do.

Lorna has a house in one of those lovely Downland villages between Lewes and Eastbourne, Eric Ravilious country, a landscape of billowing green hills, and sheep, and the abrupt white edge of England at Seven Sisters. That edge is now thronged with Chinese tourists, who arrive in unmanageable numbers to tread its crumbling paths in unsuitable footwear because, a ranger told me, it appears in a promotional advertisement in their country, and has so captured the imagination of the emerging middle class they all want to see it. I can understand why, it is a magical landscape, something to do with the quality of light and the topography and the proximity of the sea. I have always loved landscape, being in the wide fields of Northamptonshire, on the ragged west coast of Scotland, in the flat fens of Lincolnshire; we are shaped, and made, by the places we live in, and that can be equally the incident of a city street or the emptiness of watery flatlands. And there are certain landscapes to suit our moods and experience and times of life. The sea and the edge of the land have started to suit mine.

Lorna lives down a lane that runs from the prettiest village green in England, with an old market cross, and a pub, to a steep, green hill. It looks like, feels like, the heart of old England, until you realise that nearly everyone who lives there has been interviewed on Radio Four. Maybe that is old England? Her house, with a wonderful garden that climbs the slope behind it, had become for me a home from home, a place of respite when David's illness had been all but unbearable. We know it as 'Instant Ribbons', the name given it by a friend recovering from a stroke, whose speech centres throw up compelling if remote variations on the words he is looking for.

Lorna and Kevin were in the kitchen, an unlikely pair, although close, she looking like she had just come from a British Airways Platinum Club lounge, he like a gallery of eighties art, literally, for he has over the years tattooed Keith Haring figures all over himself, so strikingly, he was invited to mingle at the private view of an exhibition of his work in Mayfair, and Jeffrey Archer tried to buy him. I did not fall into their arms and sob, I did not recount what had happened, I did not share the black comedy of bereavement, I just allowed myself to fall into the routines of old friendship.

I don't remember much about the first night. We ate

something and then Lorna asked me if I wanted to watch a film and I said yes, *London Has Fallen*, a preposterous terror-ist caper in which Westminster Abbey and Tower Bridge are splendidly blown up as terrorists take out the ruling elite of the G20, but as soon as it came on I fell asleep, and woke up at the end to find Lorna and Kevin politely watching a film they both disliked.

The next day we went to Eastbourne. It was cold but bright, my favourite weather, and we walked for miles along the prom. It is the most seemly of seafronts, tarmacked, with little thatched sheds along the way in which promenaders may take shelter, and homeless people spend the night, and there are flower beds, and carefully tended shrubs, and rail-ings, and those little brightly painted beach huts, each its own castle, facing the sea.

There was nothing mannerly about the sea. The red flags were flying a warning and beyond them, pale putty green with white foam crests, the waves were crashing onto the shingle between the groynes. A liminal experience for a lim-inal moment, caught between the fastidiously ordered edge of earth, and the untouchable chaos of the sea.

We stopped for a cappuccino and a bacon butty – my appetite had recovered and seemed to be making up for lost calories – at one of the little seafront cafes there and the proprietor gave me his condolences. We sat in silence, look-ing through picture windows at the sea thrashing onto the shingle above the polite soundtrack of teaspoons and china, and then Lorna remarked that in her view Braeburns had knocked the bonnets off Granny Smiths.

We stopped at Waitrose on the way home, and I bought expensive wine, and saw someone we knew, who gave me her condolences. I was beginning to understand better why in traditional cultures the widow has a formal role, to make a passeggiata after the death, in black weeds, to receive the formal condolences of the community. I found myself rather rising to the role, adopting a look of grave solemnity in the aisles, and noticed that because of the coverage in the news, people were clocking me more than my lo-watt celebrity status normally occasions, but that look of recognition was followed almost immediately by a sympathetic, or sometimes nervous, shift. It is hard to think of anything more English than standing in Waitrose in Eastbourne, the object of distanced sympathy, by people buying forced rhubarb and salsify.

The next day was Sunday. I decided to go to church, and found one that looked congenial a few miles away. Lorna, who is a churchwarden at my last parish, did not want to come, perhaps thinking that I would prefer to be alone. I think I did, being apprehensive about going because in church we connect to the deepest and most powerful rhythms in our lives, and everyone else's lives, and if they were to swell I thought they might overwhelm me. But where better to be overwhelmed than in church? I have often come across people who have walked into one, found a seat at the back and allowed themselves to be overwhelmed. Once, in Knightsbridge, when I was locking up I came across a young woman sitting at the back who was crying bitterly. I sat next to her in silence, handing her tissues from time to time, until she was done, when she got up and left without a word, stepping through the double doors into the grand indifferent street beyond.

This church was suburban, on the edge of one of the less fashionable towns between Eastbourne and Hailsham, a congregation mostly of retired Londoners, I thought, and parents and grandparents with kids, who were running around before the service. The vicar came to say hello and introduced me to the other clergy, and I took my place in the nave, casting a professional eye, as visiting clergy always do, over the Order of Service and the set-up. There were smells and there were bells, which suits me, but if that suggests stuffy, it was not. There were Taizé chants before, sung by a small vocal group and those of us of a mind to join in, and afterwards there was a cup of tea, and football for the kids in the church hall. During the service we all prayed for David, and the congregation prayed for me, and I was glad of that although if I had expected the deep peace of the running wind, as promised by the blessing, it did not come. I felt nothing but gratefulness that there were other people there who could pray as I could not. At the Peace, when the custom is to shake hands with those around you as a sign of our reconciliation in Christ before we go to the altar, a lady came up and said, 'I'm Auntie Val, handshake or hug?' I, who rarely embrace anyone unselfconsciously, became both a giver and receiver of embraces, in those early days. I would have embraced the creature from the black lagoon had he come to pay his respects.

After lunch Lorna and Kevin and I went out in the car, and as I drove I talked about someone I had met recently, a surgeon in Syria, who had worked in a hospital through bombardments, gas attacks, and the horrors of the civil war there. He was only home a day or two when he was asked to lunch at Buckingham Palace by the Queen. She sat down next to him and asked what it was like in his hospital and he found that he could not speak, it was too much, and the Queen, noticing this, said very gently, 'Would you like to feed the corgis?' and produced a packet of treats, and they quietly fed the dogs until he regained his composure. Telling this story made me lose mine and for the first time in front of my friends I began to cry. I tried to smother it, as if it were a loss of face, which was ridiculous, but I was trying to contain the explosion, and the thought of losing control was too much for me.

I drove home later that afternoon and decided to get an Indian takeaway for supper, an unfailingly effective treat for me, and I went to pick it up from a restaurant in the next village, one of several I favour with the vicarage custom. I had to wait for a few minutes, and I saw a lady who I had sometimes spoken to before, sitting on her own. She is always dressed up, looks impeccable, and sits in the same place, with a glass of red wine, and a chicken tikka masala. One time we fell into conversation, and I discovered that she was a widow and came every Sunday evening because she always used to with her husband, same table, and then after the curry they would go to the Duke's Arms for the quiz. She still did, but without him now, and for a reminder and for a comfort she brought with her his Liverpool FC scarf, because he loved the club all his life, and because she struggles with loneliness, and because you'll never walk alone.

She invited me to sit with her. 'Sorry to hear about your friend,' she said, and I felt the shift in role, from me the vicar dispensing to her, to her the widow dispensing to me. 'What do I need to know?' I asked. 'It's really hard,' she said, 'there's no point in pretending otherwise.' Then we talked about Jürgen Klopp, who kept cropping up in conversation in these turbulent days, I do not know why.

David could not eat spicy food, his wrecked digestive system would not cope with it, nor very well with fats, so Indian takeaways, which are for me ambrosia, were so unappealing to him I could not eat them while he was around because they made him feel nauseous. I sometimes think this was partly a kickback to my impatience with his cigarette smoke, which I started to find unbearable after I gave up smoking and he did not. Sometimes we would fight not about the issues that really mattered, because these were too difficult, or too one-sided when his illness made him feeble, so we would argue instead about the smells we generated. I felt self-righteous about his smoking, because it was not only disgusting to me, but injurious to health, and he smoked like a lifer in a category A nick. He thought my smell disgusting and injurious to my heart too, fats narrowing my arteries and thickening my waist. Our different smells began to mark out different territory within the vicarage. He had a studio on the upstairs floor in which he would smoke constantly, despite what I thought to be an agreement that he would not smoke in the house. He took over the summer house, which he had built for me, and when in residence it was like an opium den in late Victorian Limehouse. I would sneak into what I was cooking ingredients I liked but he did not – we had a running battle about the place of lardons in an Italian ragu – and would sometimes sneak a curry in when he was out, only to face the music when he returned. Little arguments about food and fags replaced the bigger arguments about his lack of self-care and my failure to help him get better. They served to earth the more violent and volatile emotional impulses that would otherwise have made our lives hard to bear, but in the long term they diverted our effort and attention away from the bigger questions. You do what you have to do to get through.

In the long run this alienated us a bit. He would retreat to his fiercely defended spaces to do what he wanted to do without my spoken or unspoken criticism following him like a thundercloud, and I would sometimes disappear for lunch, go to a restaurant with a book, just so I could eat something I wanted to eat, rather than something he could eat, and this became so regular that we started to live a part of our lives separately from each other. There were times when we would both be in the vicarage all day but only meet each other in the kitchen or the garden. It became necessary to preserve our own well-being as well as our joint well-being. This changed when he went through a bad patch and needed me to look after him, and we would be close again, but crises pass and most of our lives together are lived in the day-to-day business of working out how to be together, and how to be apart.

Illness also took from us one of the things we most enjoyed, which was walking the dogs together. That took us into the country, which we both loved, and there is something about the purposefulness in walking and looking after dogs that takes your conscious attention away from the stuff that troubles you. When David was unwell he could not manage the walk and I had to do it alone, in two batches, because five dogs was too much for one person. What we loved doing when we did it together became something I found burdensome doing alone, and I missed it terribly. Chronic illness does this, not only robbing you of the joint enterprise that you loved to do, but turning the solo version of it into something you can no longer enjoy. Knowing what I know now, I would urge anyone who is looking after a partner who is seriously ill to get as much help as you can. Or as much as the ill person will permit, which in David's case was very little. He hated being ill to the point that he would prefer to pretend it was not happening, not only to me, which was very frustrating, but to his medics, who he treated with the cavalier indifference typical of another medic. More frustration.

That had all now gone, with David's death. And in the first weeks of my widowhood, in all sorts of ways, I enjoyed being alone. I enjoyed eating a chicken dhansak on a tray on my lap watching a bullet-riddled thriller, the kind of film he hated. I enjoyed not being woken up in the middle of the night by his small-hours experiments rearranging the feng shui in his studio. I enjoyed the pure air, untainted by the bitter smell of burnt tobacco. I enjoyed cooking with Scotch bonnet chillis and unctuous pork belly. All these enjoyments were almost at once extinguished by guilt, for enjoying any-thing at all now David was dead. But I could not yet believe he was dead. He was just away on an unauthorised holiday. One morning I was dozing in bed and heard the greenhouse door squeak open, and for a moment I mistook the garden-er for David. The bang/crunch of those moments is really hard, turning the savoury dish you are eating to ashes in your mouth, and filling the unsullied air with the smell of burning tyres.

Eight months into widowhood and I hear from a friend from Stratford-upon-Avon, the former flatmate who saw me knocked off my bike when we were eighteen.

Recovery then was long and slow, and in the beginning all I could do was lie in bed, unable to move, looking at a vase of daf-fodils that a flatmate had kindly brought me and placed in the window. Through the day the sunlight moved across the window and lit the flowers from left to right. It was the first time I had ever really noticed flowers, and I was captivated by them. You are alive, they said, and look at my subtlety and splendour.

The next stage was getting up and getting dressed, for which I could not bend, so had to haul up pants and socks with wire coat hangers.

Then I started to walk, slowly round the house and garden to begin with, and then along the street. I recoiled, involuntarily, from traffic going past, my body remembering the consequences of getting too close. Eventually I got back on the bike.

This time my wounds are not visible, and there is no uniform for the bereaved, the black armband, the bordered calling-card, the curtains drawn at noon. Your loss is pretty much invisible, unless people know about it, and you live and walk in the land of the not-yet bereaved, and should your wounds suddenly show people may recoil, or be struck dumb with embarrassment, or inadvertently say the wrong thing. In a supermarket between Christmas and New Year I saw someone I knew and he said he was sorry for my loss and then said, 'How was your Christmas?' I said, 'Not great,' and he blushed and apologised, and I said it was OK, and then he said that what he meant was . . . I knew what he meant, and I had not intended to reproach him, but my answer felt like a reproach, and must have hurt a bit, and caused an embarrassing and awkward exchange of words. I realised that I was a sort of walking social IED, a threat to the unwary, and with the potential to upset everyone unpredictably.

Christmas

Christmas was nearly here, and for the first time since we had been at the vicarage it was not transformed into the twinkling wonderland that David insisted on. My neighbours in the lane behind the church had put up their tasteful, white, unblinking lights, and in the evening came the sound of distant Christmas favourites, blaring from the truck made festive by the Scouts and Guides, done up with lights and a real Santa ho-ho-hoing, knocking on doors on the annual fundraising round, an upgraded version of carol singing, with less baby Jesus and more red-nosed reindeer – not that I mind much. This year the vicarage was dark, not even the Lutheran stepped candles twinkling in the window by the front door, and no one rang the bell, out of respect for my grieving state. Then there was a ring, and it was Malcolm, delivering, as he delivers every year, the Christmas cake made by his wife Marion, hands down the best Christmas cake I have ever tasted. He was kind, and I thanked him, and retreated to the kitchen where I had a Wensleydale waiting to be sliced and laid on top of the cake, a delicacy which not even grief could dull.

By day, more neighbours called too, with condolences, and a police officer came round to follow up the first visit, and Ozzie the postman rang with another bag of letters, hundreds of them, which I read in bearable batches. To break that up I went to Burton Latimer, the town next door, because I wanted to sit in a cafe anonymously and not have to deal with unmanageable levels of condolence-receiving.

But Burton Latimer too wanted to express its condolences, and a lady came and said hello and how sorry she was, and we got talking and it turned out that she and her friends, they were four, were all widows and widowers too, and they came over and we sat and talked. She and her friends had all worked for my grandfather and father at the Coles Boot Co Ltd, which was in Burton Latimer, and in its heyday employed half the town, and half of Finedon too. 'I was told off by your dad once for wonky stitching, but he was so nice about it I didn't mind. He was a lovely man.' I felt a pang of grief for my father, who had died three years earlier, and whose loss had been overlaid by David's. They gave me useful advice: 'take it steady', 'don't try to do too much too quickly', 'don't make any big decisions'. I was grateful for their concerns and helpfulness and wished them a merry Christmas. None of them wished it to me, knowing, as widows, that it would not be. 'There you are, me duck, we've genned you up a bit,' said the first lady. Widows of Burton Latimer, I thought, I salute you.

Christmas Eve. Normally this was one of the busiest days of the year, with the Children's Nativity in church, Christmas Communion visits, carols at the residential and nursing homes, and Midnight Mass, one of my favourite services of the year, when alongside our regulars we get all our irregulars, and the kids returning to parents and grandparents from university, or the military, or lives that have taken them away, often the first generation of Finedonians to have left Finedon for anything other than a world war. It was poignant for that reason, and poignant too for David, who loved Christmas like the child he had been when Christmas was cancelled, and that was poignant, and this would be the first without him, and that was unbearably poignant. So I would not be on duty with my parishioners, but away, my first Christmas off duty and away in thirty years.

The Spencers, who have some experience of public bereavement, invited me to spend Christmas with them – 'You'll be behind a wall, you'll be secure, you can come and go as you please.'

I had met Charles and Karen at a county do, the high sheriff's garden party, because Charles is a deputy lieutenant, one of the team fielded when the lord lieutenant cannot be in two places at once, and I was the high sheriff's chaplain, a role which once required the holder to say the Amen after a judge pronounced a death sentence on a felon convicted of a capital crime at the county assizes. That duty I was no longer required to fulfil, and today all it involves formally is preaching the sermon at the courts service, when the county's judiciary, under the authority of the high sheriff, meet at the parish church in Northampton and have a knees-up afterwards at the Guild Hall. There is a lot of cutlery on these occasions, swords and spurs, and chains of office, and there are buckled shoes and hose and hats, in my case a tricorn hat. I did not have a tricorn hat, so David got me one from the panto, normally Long John Silver's, and carefully unpicked the skull and crossbones from the front panel. Unfortunately its outline was clearly visible as I processed with the judges and dignitaries through All Saints' portico, sending quite the wrong message for a Christian priest.

Charles and Karen and I rather fell on each other, living in overlapping worlds through Charles's background in broadcasting and as a writer, and Karen's running a charity for children in the developing world. County dos can sometimes be duty as much as pleasure, and our affinity made for an accelerated route into friendship, and before long David and I were regular guests at Althorp.

The house is one of the most famous in England, built by a Tudor sheep magnate, upgraded over the centuries as the family too was upgraded, as Members of Parliament, Garter Knights, ennobled, re-ennobled, fielding some of the most notable names in English history, from the Duke of Marlborough to Winston Churchill, from Queen Anne's favourite courtier to Diana Princess of Wales. It had become a palace, a treasure house, dropped down in the lovely country between Northampton and Market Harborough, famous for fox hunts and its fields and hedges and holts, that still look like archetypal England, even if passing lorries on the A508 have replaced the scarlet and horn calls of the hunt.

David and I were not used to such places. On another occasion we were dining with the Buccleuchs at Boughton House, another grand county seat, even bigger than Althorp, and after dinner I realised I had left my coat in the loggia, so went to fetch it. Twenty minutes later I was lost in this vast, dark building and had to call the duke on his mobile and describe what I could make out of the tapestries on the wall so he could work out where I was and come to rescue me.

Althorp is not all fanfare. There is a grand entrance, and a state dining room, and a picture gallery, and a huge saloon with a staircase that makes the Odessa Steps look like a bar stool; but the fun is had in the library, which looks out over the deer park, one of the loveliest views in England, and feels like a club rather than a court, a place to kick back and laugh. We got the hang of Althorp after a while, its scale – grand when the occasion and the numbers demand it, public for the Literature Festival and the Food Festival, but when we got to know each other better, we came for smaller house parties, when there was no houseful, and ate in smaller and smaller rooms, until we were on intimate terms, and ate in the kitchen of the micro-Althorp they live in when no one else is there.

Over the years I had got to know the family too, and I arrived on Christmas Eve not to a houseful but Charles and Karen and four of their children. A house that size is normally staffed, but everyone gets Christmas off, apart from the security team outside, so it was just us, which presented a logistical problem. How do you find people if there is no one there to direct you? I found a way in, and eventually heard noises, and found Karen and her daughters making cupcakes in the kitchen.

Charles arrived and showed me to my room. It was where King William III had slept in 1695, and liked it so much he stayed longer than planned. I could understand why. King William's bedroom is palatial, done out in pale-blue damask, with an elegant four-poster bed, hung either side with portraits of Spencer beauties, of which there have been quite a few. There is a chaise longue at its foot and on it I plonked my luggage, a Co-op Bag for Life, which I was gratified to see was the same colour as the walls. 'Nice,' said Charles.

We had tea in the library, and Christmas cake, and I forgot I was the grieving widow by talking to the younger children about school and ponies and puppies, and one, sweetly grave as teenagers can be, said how sorry he was to hear about David, and I was very touched.

There aren't really dining rooms in grand houses. People put up tables wherever the fancy takes them and the occasion demands. A grand dinner might be by candlelight in the picture gallery, with the silver gleaming, it might be a table for four on the terrace outside, it might be in a room you had not thought would serve that purpose, or it might be, as dinner was that evening, in a room I had not even been in before, a grand room hung with portraits of an agricultural earl's favourite livestock, preferable, evidently, to his own family. Charles said it was that earl's bedroom, the custom being until the eighteenth century for the family to sleep on the ground floor, with guests upstairs. And so in the room where the third earl had slept and admired his cattle, we ate some of their descendants: beef and Yorkshire pudding, followed by cupcakes, and drank something splendid. After the littlest had gone to bed, excited that Father Christmas was en route, we talked about the carnage visited on the wildlife of Northamptonshire by hunting and shooting parties of the past. Some of these were for the benefit of the Empress of Austria, who stayed at Althorp for the hunting, and the convenient proximity of Bay Middleton, who lived at Haselbech nearby, and was considered the finest horseman in Europe. There was a portrait of her in the billiard room, sitting, tiny-waisted and side saddle, on a leaping horse. She met an unfortunate end, stabbed by an Italian anarchist beside Lake Geneva, a wound that she survived until the doctor removed her famously tight corset, which caused it to bleed uncontrollably. David and I liked staying in her favourite room, the Princess of Wales bedroom, named after the then Princess Alexandra, who came in the 1860s with another wildlife-destroying husband.

After supper, instead of going to Midnight Mass, an unbearable thought, I sat with the younger Spencers round the piano in the saloon, where the Althorp Christmas carols had happened a few days before, singers and musicians on the stairs, and we played songs, not Christmas songs, and when it was my turn I was asked to play one of my own. The only one I could remember I had written in memory of a friend who had died in the eighties, our first friend to die in the AIDS epidemic. I had gone off it, once the introduction of AZT lifted the inevitable death sentence on those infected with HIV, and thirty years later did not want to return to it particularly, but David loved it and always asked me to play it, so I played it again, in memory of him. I did not really want to, because I did not want to feel like Banquo, the ghost at their feast, my grief warping the dynamics of another's family Christmas, so I did not explain its significance. I need not have worried. The dynamics of Christmas were fine and my hosts were kind and considerate and affectionate.

I had a whisky and went to bed, and took a Zopiclone because it was Christmas Eve, always sleepless when I was a child in excited anticipation of the day ahead, and sleepless now because grief is like reverse anticipation, keeping you awake with sudden and vivid memories. I thought of the former occupant of this bed, who I supposed never imagined he would be King William III of England, having fought it disastrously twenty years earlier, and I wondered if he ever sighed, looking out of the windows of state bedrooms, feeling nostalgic for the Prinsenhof at Delft, in the middle of one of the liveliest towns in Europe at the end of the Dutch Golden Age.

It knocked me out, and I slept so well I did not wake until after eight, late for me. When I came down everyone was up and had fallen on the cairns of exquisitely wrapped presents that lay under the enormous Christmas Tree. Charles made me breakfast and then I watched as the opening of presents continued, neither receiving nor giving, for I am a terrible present-giver even to those I owe presents and asked particularly to be excused. Charles asked me what I wanted to do and I said go to church, and he said that he probably wouldn't, having done duty at the estate carol service, and that was quite enough religion to see him through the Octave of the Nativity and quite far into 2020.

I decided to go to All Saints in Northampton, the principal church in our county town, where the rector is a friend of mine and a contemporary at theological college. He is now a rising star, rightly so, and the church was full and splendid, with smells, spectacularly administered by a thurifer who swung the censer effortlessly through 360 degrees (a manoeuvre so smoky it is saved only for the grandest festivals), and bells, and a robed choir, and I sat at the end of a pew trying not to be conspicuous, but being conspicuous. I was fine until the exchange of peace, when my friend came over and embraced me and I let out an *ouff*, which needed letting out, partly because I was full of grief at that moment, and partly because the chasuble he wore was so stiff with orphreys and bullion it was like embracing a suit of renaissance armour.

I have infringed two of the most strictly enforced regulations David imposed on the vicarage. First, I have parked my bike in the hall. In fact I have parked THREE bikes in the hall. Second, I have used his carving knife for things other than carving. I have done so with an alacrity I think at first deliberately disrespectful to his memory, as if I am angry with him for dying. But I'm not angry with him. I think it's imagining how furious he would be at these two terrible crimes – it's so intense it slows his rate of fade.

I did not hang around after the service, just said goodbye to the rector, and drove back to Althorp. It was a bright, clear and cold morning, and I parked at the back and went for a walk through the park. It was perfectly quiet, and perfectly still, save the bleating of sheep, and the quacking of waterfowl, round the curiously named Round Oval, a small lake with a little island in the middle. It is famous for being the burial place of Princess Diana, Charles's older sister. I knew her a little before I knew Charles, for we were involved in the same charity in the eighties and nineties, and I would see her sometimes at receptions. I cannot say I knew her really; I met her a few times, when she was perhaps the most recognisable person in the world, and for that reason one of the most trespassed on. Her burial, on an island in the middle of a lake, behind the estate's walls, was considered necessary at the time because of the intensity of interest in her death, and that if she were to be interred in the Spencer tombs at Great Brington church, alongside her father and nineteen generations of ancestors, it might become impossible to manage those who would want to visit. So the Bishop of Peterborough consecrated the water-girt mound of earth, and after her extraordinary funeral the cortège passed through the famous gates to the park, and she to her final resting place.

Or not: almost immediately there was a rumour that she had been secretly interred with her ancestors in the church by midnight, a story straight out of romantic fiction, but then so much of her life seemed to come straight out of romantic fiction.

The intensity of interest around her was extraordinary in life and extraordinary in death too. I remember in the days after the accident walking along the queues of people waiting to write in the Book of Remembrance in St James's Palace. They queued for hours, days, and wrote pages and pages. So many people wanted to write so many things there were Books of Remembrance everywhere. There was even one in Tesco's in Kettering. I understood now how we want to attach our bereavements to bigger bereavements, and to this, the biggest bereavement of all, so that our stories are taken up in this big story, given visibility and importance, and we need that because we fear and know that the death which gradually erases them will come for us and erase us too.

Back then, Diana, on whom we'd hung all our griefs, to amplify them, so that others would see and hear, seemed inextinguishable. I watched the funeral on television, from the beginning of the journey from outside Buckingham Palace to Westminster Abbey, the crowds deep on either side, and tears from old and young, men and women. I was thrilled by Charles's eulogy, moved by the John Tavener piece, 'Song for Athene', when the coffin was carried out and put in a hearse and began its last journey through London, and on to Northamptonshire, and to here, more than twenty years ago now.

I sat looking out at the island, wondering how you got there, if you wanted to. Then I saw a rowing boat tethered to the side and thought I might row out, but the likelihood of falling in, on a cold Christmas morning, and having to explain to my host that I had been attempting to land on the island where his sister is buried made me reconsider. There is also something about her isolation there that is impressive. The romantic fiction would have it that there she is, finally, beyond the intrusive gaze of anyone, paparazzi, tourists, me. But I also think she was distant in life too because of the extraordinary existence she had lived since she married the heir to the throne. On the other side of the island there is a little neo-classical temple, with her face in silhouette, and name on it, indelibly. But that death, so noticed by the world, had begun to fade too; the numbers visiting the Diana exhibition at Althorp had decreased to the point when it was no longer sensible to continue. When it had opened, in the first weeks of operation the teaspoons in the cafeteria, marked with the Spencer S, were stolen in their thousands.

David would soon be forgotten. Not by me, ever, nor by those who loved him most, but by the world. It was already happening, deleted from people's contacts, unresponsive on Twitter and Facebook, and, now I had the death certificate, the Tell Us Once algorithms were deleting David from the financial sector, from government; the erasure was remorseless. Six months later, I still cannot bring myself to press delete when David's name comes up on Twitter and Facebook and my phone.

That could all wait for now. It was Christmas Day. The library looked like Glastonbury on the day of departure; there were piles of wrapping paper, ribbons strewn like seaweed at low tide, and treacherously underfoot, but invisible, numberless stocking-filler toys that if not picked up threatened to damage the dog and the Dyson. I made a patchy effort to tidy up, not exactly singing for my supper but I wanted to do something in response to the generosity and hospitality of my hosts. We reconvened for lunch in my favourite room in the house, an anteroom to the picture gallery, a lovely cube hung with green damask, in which a Spencer relative had died of the smallpox in the reign of Queen Victoria and its contents thereafter burned and replaced with bits and pieces from Spencer House in London, so glossy and metropolitan rather than the cattle market of the third earl's bedroom. It is a mini picture gallery in itself, and has a painting I especially like of Robert Arnauld by Philippe de Champaigne, one of my favourite painters, a Jansenist, one of my favourite sects, and a regular, with Blaise Pascal, at the convent at Port-Royal at the end of the seventeenth century. Arnauld in this portrait looks like Malcolm Rifkind dressed as a Jesuit, and I had always thought it was a painting of a cleric until I looked closer and found out who he was – a finance minister for Marie de Medici, a poet and, ironically, a persecutor of Jesuits. He was a former Solitaire of Port-Royal, where he had spent thirty years pruning fruit trees, and became a renowned expert in this art. In his hand he holds a glowing treasure, which I at first thought was a golden orb but on inspection turned out to be an orange. I remembered admiring it once with the historian Dan Jones who remarked that it anticipated the Christingle, which made me laugh for a whole day.

Lunch started traditional, turkey and so forth, and ended contemporary, Karen and her daughter more used to LA diets than English stodge, and we talked to those of age about the extraordinarily complicated and perilous sexual mores of Generation X, which was eye-opening and satisfactorily different from the arguments about the merits of the baroness in *The Sound of Music* which David and I would normally have got on to by the Christmas pudding. In the middle of this one of the boys said, as an aside, that I was like one of the family, and it stopped me dead. I was so touched that he said it, and if I were in the market for an alternative family the Spencers would do very nicely, but it also reminded me that I was now a soloist. David had put so much into making us a unit, a family, a dynasty, not quite the Spencers, or even the Waltons, but populous with dachshunds, and observant of traditions, and with a future, and solid. That had now all gone, at a stroke, and when the awareness of this hit me, usually when it was not expected, I would think, and still do, 'Poor Tom's a-cold', and that I had been evicted from home and was wandering the blasted heath with nowhere to go, nothing to do,

I left after tea. Charles walked me to the door and said, 'I know we said no presents, but I want you to have this,' and gave me a limited edition copy of his history of the Spencer family, beautifully bound in blue leather, and signed for me.

On the way home I called in at my mother's. She had been on her own, bar carers, for Christmas, my two other brothers away with their spouses' families. Normally she would come to us, and when it got too difficult for her to come to us after church we would go to her, with presents and cards and as many of the Christmas delicacies she could manage. Now it was just me and her, with a cup of tea and a mince pie, watching nonsense on television, with the ghost of Christmas past occasionally hovering over us as we remembered when I was a child, and she a mother of three, cooking for a dozen on Christmas Day, and another dozen on Boxing Day, of heroic catering, and the best presents, and charades, and family traditions. Life, towards its end, gets thin. The more I see of it, the more I feel sympathy for Ebenezer Scrooge, the unredeemed Scrooge, who seems to me a far more plausible character than the creaky, too-late Santa at the end. There is no pardon for Tiny Tim in life, when earth is hard as iron and water like a stone.

We needed God to become incarnate, for we are not able to thaw winter ourselves. And at a cost, the holly berry reminds us, we are unable to bear.

'There are no words . . .' but there is music. I most fully inhabit my grief when I listen to music, one or two pieces that connect my thinking self with my feeling self. It is Joni Mitchell's 'A Case of You', which I sang to him as he lay dying.

It is 'Casta Diva' from Bellini's opera Norma, *which David loved, and when his hardships were unendurable he would listen over and over to Maria Callas singing it with the suicidal intensity I cannot listen to any more. Give me Joan Sutherland singing it now, like a woman thinking of her pension rather than her epitaph. We went to see it once at Covent Garden, guests of a generous friend with a box, and David was late, and I was fuming, but he made it in time for the aria and at the end shouted with a grossly overcooked Italian accent 'Bravissima!' into an auditorium up to that moment silent with appreciation. I was so angry with him I could barely be civil, but all he was doing was enjoying himself.*

The piece that makes me feel his loss most keenly is Vaughan Williams' organ prelude 'Rhosymedre', played at David's funeral, not because I associate it with that, but because the tune, an old Welsh hymn, sometimes goes by the English name Lovely, and David was to me inexpressibly lovely, and in spite of everything in his life which was tough and hard, and in spite of what we suffered together, he made my life lovely, as no one else could, and never will. It slows in the last couple of bars, and resolves over a deep bass pedal note, which fades in the giant acoustic of a church and he is gone.

I have always loved Boxing Day, the run-up and run-down to great events preferable to me than the event itself. When I was a child it was beagling in the morning, with the least dangerous beagle pack in England, but not something I would pursue now; and lunch and tea with the cousins. Cousin lunch had faded away with the generation before ours, upon which we relied for organisation, and because church comes first for the ordained, and I regretted this because I love my cousins, and their children, now grown up, and the family story extending in all sorts of interesting ways, into Formula 1, and veterinary practice on the Argentinian pampas, and having kids, and the Candy brothers' deluxe developments, and dentistry. My generation, the first to move away, the first to scatter, the first to skip the annual gatherings. At least as a vicar I had a good excuse, the marathon of Christmas Day justifying Boxing Day off, apart from in those accursed years when it falls on a Sunday.

It was not a Sunday and I had nothing to do, but quite liked that because I knew I needed to tend my wounds, which I wanted to do alone, and huddle with the dogs. Someone sent me an article about the Kubler Ross theory of the stages of grief, a metric I have always found a bit doubtful, if only for the too obvious convenience of it offering something useful to say in the face of brute fate. In my experience, grief – my own and other people's – does what it wants to do, it is not obedient to psychological patterning, or theological argument, or the opinion of anyone, least of all you. It comes when it comes, and it goes when it goes, and it can snatch you out of relative composure with unpredictable and irresistible force. And it is all yours, and no one else's. I remember in the eighties when a former lover died of AIDS someone telling me at the funeral that it was OK to feel what I was feeling, and I thought, Where do you get off giving people permission to feel? I suppose what lies underneath that is the unquenchable desire to defeat it, in one way or another, through denial, through miraculous reversal, through parallel universes, through spectral existence. A bit rich coming from you, you may think, but Christianity does not offer you a palliative or an escape from this. On the contrary, it insists on the fact of death; without it, there's no hope of a new life beyond that last horizon. For some that means Aunt Phyllis and the family spaniel bounding towards them across the springing meadows of eternity to greet them. For others, me included, it conjures no cast of best-loved characters, no misty shore, or flowery field, but something more like geometry. I have always liked Botticelli's illustrations for *The Divine Comedy*, which begin busily in Inferno, thronged and detailed, hell being so much easier to imagine than its alternatives, then move to Purgatory, which is less busy, and more strange, and end in heaven, with the pilgrim floating around concentric circles.

We cannot know God. We can look in that direction, if we are not blinded by its light, a strobe flashes to illuminate for a split second the darkness of this world, something from deep in memory fires up with a significance we did not see at the time, but, to paraphrase St Thomas Aquinas, we do not know what we are talking about, so whatever we say is a shadow of a shadow. I know that my redeemer liveth, and that at the latter day I will too, but it will be in a form that we can only imagine, and when we press that the detail falls away until all we are left with is light, and line, and πr^2.

Also, Christians, like everyone else, need to grieve when they lose the ones they love. I have never been of the school that thinks our priesthood obliges us to offer business as usual, and bury our mothers and our husbands and our children dry-eyed and level-voiced in the sure and certain hope. Some do, and good luck to them, but I could not, would not. I have no doubt in the mercy and generosity of God, nor in the promise of more to come, and wonderfully, but I needed other people to do the honours so that I could honour David with my grief.

Our narrowboat is moored on a bend in the river Nene next to the village where I grew up. The Nene Valley is at its best in the stretch between Wellingborough and Oundle and the plan was to have somewhere to get away to within fifteen minutes of the vicarage. David turned its renovation and makeover into a major project. He completely redid the interior and made it beautiful, another example of his irresistible and restless habit of making a Festival of Booths wherever he went. Next to the boat he built a boathouse named Cul na Shee, *Scots Gaelic for* Nook of Peace, *the name of the house we rent every year in Kintyre.*

Both the boat, when it was done, and the boathouse were presented to me for my delight, and they were beautiful, but they were also uninhabitable. This was partly because David's relentless accumulation of dogs made it impractical to spend any time there; not even the most resilient bargee would keep five dachshunds on a forty-two-foot narrowboat. It was also partly because I could not bear the smell of cigarette smoke and David smoked with such extraordinary commitment I sometimes felt he did so to fumigate me; and because – the most important reason – it looked to me like his space, and the friends he made down there his friends. I think he needed this, but that need was in tension with his desire to please me, and to create a space where we could be together as we were when we were in Scotland.

It is a hot summer's day, six months since he died, and the river is at its loveliest when the swallows are on the wing, and the ducks and coots and moorhen and paddleboarders glide past. It is time to see what it feels like to be there. Since David's death it has been looked after by a friend on the boat opposite, and another friend has lived in it during lockdown after she returned from Guatemala, an epic story of repatriation, with nowhere to go thanks to rules about who got to household, a new verb I have just invented, with whom.

It is good, at first, to step on board, into something that is so him, from the stained glass he commissioned for its windows, in the owl motifs that had become his sigil, to the Homes and Gardens *fittings in the bathroom and the galley. It is also smoke free, no phantom fag smell to perturb me, and tidy. I make a cup of tea, then play the accordion, 'Ye Banks and Braes o' Bonnie Doon', one of the tunes we used to play together, David on fiddle. That is good too, it feels positive, a reminder of an addition rather than subtraction; but then I lie on the sofa look-ing up into the sky, watching the swallows criss-cross in flight and a puffy white cloud sails very slowly by. Radio Three is on and it plays the violin and piano piece* Spiegel im Spiegel *by Arvo Pärt, a simple and beautiful piece that we used to play too. Sadness takes me, not the piercing loss that the early days of grief brings, but a slow, building wave. I ache for him, and that is bad, but it also invites in regret and guilt – the handmaidens of a death like David's – and I feel in that moment, full force, that I should have been kinder, loved him more strongly, made him happier. I could have done, but I did not, because I was too self-absorbed, and there is nothing I can do about it now.*

The Lamentation in Rama

It was the weekend again and I could not bear to be at home and to hear the church bell tolling, summoning me to something I could not yet face, so I arranged to spend it with our friends, Jon and Mike, in Dorset. Jon and I met thirty-five years ago in Islington, where we both lived, and walked our dogs in the park. David and I had been guests at their civil partnership and they were the witnesses and only guests at ours, so in rites of union we had lived in parallel.

My first defence against being overwhelmed by grief was organisation. I had registered David's death, I had the death certificate, I had made arrangements with the funeral directors, I had booked the cricket club and the caterers, and decided, in the rush of momentum, the next thing I needed to do was arrange a headstone. I had found a stonemason who specialised in making them, Fergus Wessel, works of art as well as monuments, and with a small detour I could call in at his workshop in the Cotswolds on the way to Dorset.

I emailed ahead and he said come to lunch. Fergus's studio and workshop are next to his house down a long lane in a small village. As I arrived at the path someone came out, a little younger than me, thin and wiry, with the faint suggestion of an unorthodox British army officer about him. It was Fergus, who greeted me and invited me into his studio, an old barn. One of the guys he works with was kneeling on a headstone which lay flat on a worktable, looking like a Victorian dentist extracting a wisdom tooth from a supine patient, only he was working with minute and intense concentration, chiselling with fine judgement an inscription into the stone. The verticals and serifs, order and line and pattern, yielded to subtle flourishes, ligatures, a swell in the curve of a hanging figure 3, a reassertion of the organic in the mineral substrate that made me think of fossils, the imprint of biology appearing like a surprise in the sterile grain of stone.

We sat at a table and Fergus took out a notebook and asked me what I wanted. I said two headstones, one for him, one for me, companion pieces, that will stand side by side when we lie side by side in the churchyard at Grafton Underwood. I wanted simple, plain, Welsh slate, for I know from churchyards that slate lasts longest, holds best the impression of a name, and the name recorded thus endures through years, decades, centuries.

Fergus made some notes and then said, gently, 'When did David die, Richard?'

I said, 'Last week.'

He closed his notebook and said, 'Come back in six months.'

'I know what I want.'

'I'm sure you do, and I like it very much, but it takes time.'

'I want to get on with it.'

'Not only for you, for the grave as well. It takes time to settle. You cannot install a headstone until it has.'

I thought of Stanley Spencer's general resurrection, of the graves of the churchyard at Cookham giving forth their dead, in their turn-ups and round specs and pinnies, and of the totentanz in churchyards like mine, where the dead have been buried since long before Christianity arrived, and the earth is never entirely still, and over the centuries its cargo of bones shifts and settles and shifts again.

'Come and have some lunch.'

We sat at the kitchen table and his wife made soup and bread and cheese and we talked theology, which I was not expecting, and got so involved in a discussion about the nature of scriptural authority that they forgot it was time to pick up the kids from school and there was rather a rushed departure.

During my solitary, grief-nursing trip to Wales after David's funeral, one morning I leave the dogs in the cottage and cycle into Hay-on-Wye. It is a town we used to visit sometimes, on the way to see friends in Powys, and David would spend a fortune there on Welsh blankets from the kind of shop which depends on the custom of English second-homers and visitors and festival-goers, who strew the beds of Islington and Henley-on-Thames with textiles originally made as presents for newly-weds in Caernarvon and Capel Dewi. The blanket shop, though lit, is shut, and I feel like Tiny Tim peering from the cold street through the poulterer's window; but Hay is famous for bookshops too, and I spent the morning working my way through them. I found in one a lovely edition of Francis Kilvert's diaries. He was curate at nearby Clyro in the 1870s, undistinguished in clerical life, but a wonderful writer, and his accounts of ministering in the villages and farms of Radnorshire, of disappointment in love, and a winning enthusiasm for nude swimming, are as celebrated as Parson Woodforde's diaries a century earlier.

Then I discover, on an overfilled shelf in a dark corner of a shop that creaks like a ship, a lovely edition of Tennyson's In Memoriam, *the long and beautiful and passionate poem of 1850 he wrote for the then - perhaps forever - love of his life, Arthur Hallam, who died at twenty-two. I have always loved it, but this edition, bound in vellum, seemed so timely, so lovely, that I buy it for an enormous price and with a feeling of destiny.*

I can barely read since David died. A novel looks like the north face of the Eiger, non-fiction, which I read more easily, as sterile as IKEA instructions; but poetry, especially a poem about two men in love and loss, might be readable, might crack the lock on my grief, and I can howl for David alone in the cottage on a high ridge overlooking a valley.

I ritualise the reading, light a fire and candles, pour a whisky, settle, and, ten stanzas in, read:

Forgive my grief for one removed,
  Thy creature, whom I found so fair.
  I trust he lives in thee, and there
I find him worthier to be loved.

I cannot read any more, conventional pieties are unbearable, and I put the book down on the floor and leave it there.

The next day the sun is shining and I go out on the bike again, and when I get back discover that Pongo, all but tooth-less, has used what's left to chew off the calfskin binding, biltong for dachshunds, and ruined the book less than a day after I bought it.

I put it on the fire and watch it cremate slowly, leaving a sort of ghost of itself, pages still distinct but the palest greys, and when I touch them they dissolve into ash.

I stopped for tea too – sounds a little Emily Dickinson – further down the road, with some old friends, Piers and Paula, who live in Wiltshire. I am godfather to one of their sons, Luke, who is now grown up and was away with his girlfriend. His older brother, Sam, is a golden child of a golden marriage, his parents handsome and elegant in the swashbuckling way of the English officer class. As a baby Sam was so beautiful he was the star of a Body Shop advert, picked for that role by Jon, awaiting my arrival for supper, when he was the head of design there.

Sam is now tall, and charming, and brilliant, and at the Foreign Office, and I felt that sudden realisation of time going that those without children feel when they encounter the now adult children of their friends, who are no longer asking you to be an aeroplane but sending things in diplomatic bags where geopolitics are most lively.

I think now what I was doing in these weeks after David's death was trying to reconnect the intersecting parts of my life which had become disconnected by ordination, and civil partnership, and his illness, which had made it impossible to sustain the friendships and gatherings of the clans which had been so much part of my life before David and the dog collar and dogs. I had always felt bad about this, life choices of necessity relegating former priorities, and I missed them, not only because I loved them, but because as you live on you realise we are not so much the authors of our lives but a library of other people.

And sometimes these aspects of ourselves, once discovered, may be surprising. I had met Piers and Paula in the nineties, friends of a friend, when I was coming out of the darkest period of the HIV epidemic, and from the profoundly formative years of gay liberation, activism, and pop stardom, which the eighties had so unexpectedly brought. Piers and Paula were not of that world – they were the only people I had ever met who played polo, which was one of the reasons I liked them so much – and, to put this bluntly, unconsciously I think I wanted to form relationships with people who were not going to die. We became good friends, I would often stay with them, we went away on holiday together, I became godfather to Luke. A marker of the difference of my life in their world is that they call me Dick, rather than Richard, or Tricky, or Elsie, or Father Richard, the names I go by, or have gone by, in other incarnations. I have always liked the non-overlapping magisteria of separate social worlds, and have always reserved the right to live slightly different lives in them. Piers' and Paula's world was the first in which I found my feet among people in which different values, sometimes fundamental values, prevailed. They are both from army families: Paula the daughter and the sister of brigadiers, and the only person I know who still unselfconsciously refers to herself as 'one'; Piers a former Gurkha officer turned City derivatives trader (something to do with potatoes), and the first Eurosceptic I ever had reason to take seriously, had wisdom and virtue in ways I had not really encountered before, and I find their friendship enriching.

I walked round the garden with Paula; I had made the same tour twenty-five years ago when she was planting it. Showing me now the magnificence of her works, I remembered that the last time I had seen them I was coming back from Winchester where I had been preaching at the cathedral, and planned to stay the night, but not long after I arrived I got a call to say that David was unwell and I had to leave early to get home for him.

I felt a sudden pang, and an unworthy pang, that their life was measured by a garden growing to maturity, and their sons growing up and conquering their worlds, and mine by illness and loss. Self-pity is neither attractive nor helpful, and while I would allow a moment or two of indulgence to those in extremis, and to myself, it is a good idea to move on as quickly as you can.

I said goodbye and headed south-west to Jon and Mike's

and got there in time for supper. They live in what looks like a short street of houses. It was indeed once a short street of houses for farm labourers, down a lane past the church, which Jon with his limitless appetite for doing things up had made into one, long, house. Jon looks like a designer, tall and blond and well turned out, and his husband, Mike, is yin to that yang, shorter, stockier and browner, a mother from Burma, a father from Wales.

I had not seen Jon and Mike properly for years, our visits to them another casualty of the church calendar, dog care, and David's health, and they were part of the beginning of our life together, and I wanted to be there not only for their company but also because it was fitting that they should be part of the end of our life together.

It was dinner time when I arrived. Jon had roasted a chicken and poured lots of wine, and we ate and drank. Then, in a curious repeat of what I had done at Lorna's house the weekend before, I lay on the sofa and tried to watch a film – *Paddington 2* – and drink whisky, but fell asleep instead. Jon gently woke me and we went to bed, and I was suddenly filled with grief and remorse. I texted a friend, a psychotherapist, and splurged to her and she suggested I talk to someone professional and offered some names. I also took to Twitter, in grief, and people were kind except one, a man I do not know, who told me to pull myself together and do my job, meaning be a priest, an insensitive thing to say to someone grief-stricken, and stupid too, because I was in that moment in need of receiving care, not giving it.

By now wide awake, I found in a pile of books chosen by the host for my delight and instruction Anne Glenconner's memoir of her life of privilege and drama and comedy and tragedy. In one chapter she describes her days as chatelaine of Glen House in the Borders. Her husband's uncle, the aesthete

Stephen Tennant, came to stay but thought the purple of the heather on the hills so vulgar his host had hundreds of blue paper flowers planted among it until it was a shade to his taste. They also gave him two caimans from Trinidad as a present which he kept on a hotplate in the dining room lest they miss the balmy climate of their Caribbean home.

Eventually I fell asleep, and had strange dreams – they recurred for a while – discovering a flat in London I had forgotten about, or forgotten to sell, and it had been empty, with the central heating on, for thirty years, and was full of incredibly delicate and ornate wasps' nests, and was dingy and dowdy and desolate, and I was sad about that, and then remembered that it was also like a lottery win, an unexpected fortune waiting to be realised.

I woke up feeling better. Jon and I went for a walk with the dog in nearby Grovely Wood. It was cold, and the sky was blank and white, but it was not raining, even though there had been a lot of rain and the ground was squelching underfoot and the air had that distinctive half-good, half-bad odour of rotting leaves. A Roman road passes through the woods, and we walked it and talked about David, whom Jon and Mike had both liked very much, and he them. We used to go on holiday together, to their place in Italy in the summer, and once in winter to a house on Dartmoor that I had rented, and the snow started to fall thickly as we arrived, and the thermometer dropped to minus fifteen, and we were trapped in a medieval house with an enormous fireplace that efficiently funnelled heat immediately out of the building and into the freezing night. After three days, with supplies running low, we heard a motor outside and were hailed by a man in a four-wheel drive Land Rover. 'I'm going to try to get to Okehampton,' he said, 'do you need anything urgently?' 'Yes,' I said, 'flat-leaf parsley.'

Jon took me off the path to show me a very strange beech tree, like something from folklore. It was set apart from its neighbours and garlanded with peculiar ornaments, which I took at first to be dog walkers' poo bags, which people unaccountably hang on trees rather than take home. But these were not poo bags, they were charms, and dolls, and spells, and prayers, and sometimes, Jon told me, gifts of money, hung there to propitiate old gods, I suppose. Maybe the gods never went away? The trees are said to commemorate the Grovely Witches, the four Handsel sisters who arrived in Wilton in 1737 from Denmark. There was an outbreak of smallpox, which killed a hundred and thirty people, and these women, foreigners, were accused of being responsible for practising witchcraft. A mob came to their house and dragged them to the woods where they were beaten to death and buried in four separate graves at a distance from each other so they could not in death conspire against their judges and executioners. Four beeches marking their graves magically grew and stand there to this day, the largest hung with strange offerings. I could not stop thinking about the terror of the last moments of these women, and wondering if they understood what was happening, and that they were going to die for crimes they did not commit, and who would be first?

When we got home, Jon took me to see the little church in the village, which he had decorated for Christmas to a degree of exceptional festive splendour its tiny congregation must have oohed and aahed at; but then he told me that the tiny congregation was not really apple-cheeked farmers' wives and tweedy retired colonels but included the Commissioner of the Metropolitan Police and a Law Lord. The English rural idyll: weekend retreats for people whose birthdays are in the paper, and the parish church made over by Franco Zeffirelli.

In the evening Jon cooked and Mike took me to Tisbury, where the art gallery Messum's has a country outpost. Art installations in rural locations produce a deflating effect in me, and normally within ten minutes of arriving at a sculpture park I want to go home. Not so here. The artist Bruce Munro had set up in the tithe barn, a handsome thirteenth-century structure, ancient and intact, its trusses, holding up the cruck roof, exposed like ribs. Stepping into it from the gathering darkness of the night I felt like Jonah in the belly of the whale. Suddenly a *fiat lux* – a river of light – appeared, flowing from one end of the barn to the other, and returning, then returning again. It was made from thousands of old CDs that had been fastened together like fish scales, and blue and white and green lights played on it, rippling, reflective, and submarine. I thought of the Rhinegold, protected by its watery maidens, a treasure at once elusive but irresistible, and I felt I was Alberich at the water's edge, unable to transform himself and step from one to the other, and have life.

The next day, Sunday, Mike and I went to Salisbury Cathedral for the Eucharist. Churches, even cathedrals, offer skeleton services between Christmas and New Year, the choristers allowed home after Evensong on Christmas Day, the clergy engaging unsmiling neutral as the last descant of the last carol fades. I love Salisbury, not so much for the famous 123-metre spire – such a draw for tourists from the Russian federation – but for its font. Not an arcane font but installed in 2008, looking like an upside-down Canterbury cap, water flat and reflective on its surface, pouring away at its corners to the four points of the compass; it is the first thing to greet people as they enter, a reminder that through its waters, freely given, we enter not only a building but the faith that put it up. I dipped my fingers in it as we passed and crossed myself, good Anglo-Catholic habit, and we were directed to seats in the choir, there being not so many takers for the holy mysteries on the Sunday between Christmas and New Year.

On 29 December we usually keep St Thomas Becket's day in tribute to the martyred archbishop, whom I especially liked for his peevishness, banishing the nightingales from Otford because their singing kept him awake and making all the townspeople of Strood grow tails because they were unkind to his horse. But this year 29 December was a Sunday, which displaces even the mightiest of saints, and the gospel reading for this Sunday, the first after Christmas, was Matthew's account of the massacre of the innocents, a brutal reminder that the peace of the illuminated crib is an interlude in a story of darkness and violence. In Rama, the voice of lamentation, mothers grieving their dead children, untempered by music, was a hard breakfast, and I was glad the service was short. On the way out one of the clergy stopped me and said how sorry she was to hear about David and it turned out that she was a recent widow too, and we swapped notes, secular wisdom imparted in a sacred space.

I got home that night, returning to the sound of dogs scampering downstairs to see me, their invariably enthusiastic welcome both a tonic and a blow. Who doesn't like an enthusiastic welcome? But I had also a hard reality to face about their future, and their innocence of what had happened, and what was going to happen, was hard to own.

I spent the evening watching television and eating Indian takeaway, fiery comfort, the dogs curled up on the sofa, and then we went to bed, two on, the older long-haired ones, and three in, the two short-haired brown minis, and the most recent arrival a blue-grey short-haired standard. Sleeping with your dogs on the bed, in the bed, horrifies some – my mother thinks it barbarian – but once you cross that Rubicon there really is no going back, and for me, in a bed suddenly so much emptier than it had been, they were immensely comforting. Audrey, in particular, one of the brown short-hairs, tucked herself into the crook of my knees as tightly as she could, for her benefit and for mine, and as I fell asleep would from time to time lick my feet.

Mrs W, widow of the parish, and a stalwart support in my early days of widowhood, comes round with panackelty, a sort of corned beef hash as made by her foremothers in the colliery towns of Co. Durham. It is absolutely delicious, as is her summary of the advice in lifestyle magazines dealing with grief, which she describes as 'bollocks'.

I had another appointment with the funeral directors the following day, to drop off David's grave clothes, or rather burial vestments. As a priest myself, I know my way round that particular wardrobe, but I was nevertheless very nervous about choosing something for him to wear, for it was a reversal of the normal configuration. David commanded all aspects of my wardrobe, from socks, which I once attempted to wear with sandals to his limitless horror, to a complete suite of outfits for a transatlantic crossing. He was beyond particular himself and in his quest to find suitable shoes for a non-black tie evening at sea had acquired about as many pairs as Imelda Marcos, which he would attempt to conceal from me by stowing them in unlikely places. I, however, was pickier than him in vesture, the inheritance of my background and training in churches higher than his, and I did not want to overdress him for eternity with the maniple and apparelled amice that were customary at my former parish. The happiest I had ever seen David in vestments was when we were on pilgrimage in the Holy Land, when he would wear a simple white cassock-alb and a priest's stole, dress down, but with the essentials.

That would do for eternity, I decided, and I found his cassock-alb on a hanger in his wardrobe. I took it down, and saw on the empty hanger a sticker with his name on in his handwriting, and I was suddenly hit by grief, the blows which come when you find continuing existence in the things that were theirs: name tags, voicemail messages, incoming mail.

Then I went to find his ordination stole, which I had given him, a lovely thing in white damask and red and gold embroidery, made by Watts & Co, one of the ecclesiastical suppliers in Tufton Street behind Westminster Abbey, the Church of England's Diagon Alley. I could not find it. I looked everywhere, or everywhere accessible without a forensic search team, and I did not have time for that because his body was going to be dressed and sealed in the coffin ready for his arrival in church. I decided to dress him in mine, which was given me by my parents when I was ordained, a rather different sort of stole by a contemporary embroiderer, who had foreseen the direction of my ministry and incorporated sequins.

I could not find that either. I think David had probably used it and not replaced it on its hanger, a habit he was notorious for, and the irony of looking for a stole to bury him in that he had already buried in impenetrable junk made me laugh. So I found another white stole, a simple one with a cross at each end, to equip him for active ministry come the general resurrection, when the graves will give forth their dead and we will know each other again, only as God intended us rather than as creatures of time and decay. For this he would need also the basic tools of the priest's trade, a chalice and paten, the silver cup and plate from which we distribute the bread and wine of communion made holy by Jesus as his body and blood.

I gave him mine, a lovely Edwardian set, Arts and Crafts, that I had found in the same shop in Diagon Alley when I was priested. I laid his cassock-alb on the bed, with the stole in place, and crossed the arms in front, and placed the chalice and paten on it, and put with it the last overnight bag I ever packed for him, with clericals and socks and shoes, and at the funeral director's discreet, but firm, insistence, a pair of pants. Do people sometimes forget to include these, obliging their departed loved ones to go commando into that good night?

Michael, the back-office brother, took me into his office and I handed over the overnight bag, and Jonathan, the ops brother, promised me that he would make him look just right. There were two more issues to discuss. First, media enquiries. Since the notice had gone up on the website they had received some enquiries, including one from ITV News who wanted to report the funeral. Would that be all right with me, and would I be interviewed? It was fine with me, but I did not want to be interviewed. Understood. That made me begin to worry about numbers. Finedon parish church is relatively large, big enough to seat five hundred, and I had not thought until that moment we might not have enough space. What if everyone who followed David on Twitter, several thousand, wanted to come, how would we manage if there were not enough places to seat them? Michael was not worried about this, with the clairvoyance of the professional, like a caterer, sensing that we would have room enough, and realising that in grief's madness we cannot reliably tell our shoe size let alone a funeral congregation.

The second issue was flowers. Irene wanted yellow roses, and yellow roses we would have, but try to sort a florist between Christmas and New Year, when most are shut, and when there are no deliveries? I remembered talking to a florist who had been asked to do the funeral of a boy who had died on Christmas Eve in a car accident, and she had got up in the middle of the night to drive to New Covent Garden Market, load up, and drive back to be ready for the church opening.

We managed to find one who looked at the back of the cupboard and located enough yellow roses to make a pedestal and provide one for everyone going to the burial, which would just be family and close friends. I remembered in my last parish doing a funeral when fifty thousand pounds had been spent on flowers, too much, not only for the extravagance of the cost, I thought, but because it made me feel like we were in a hothouse at Kew.

There was also a logistical issue. David's coffin was coming into church the night before the funeral, where I would receive it, the only liturgy I would officiate at, with only family and his closest friends in attendance; but we already had a funeral booked in the morning, an eleven o'clock preceding his at two, so I arranged to meet Jonathan in the morning after David's arrival, move him to the vestry in the north transept for the duration of the first funeral, and then move him back in time for his.

I felt suddenly that I was done. That was enough funeral arranging for me. I needed to leave it in the hands of others. I came home and got into scampers and was thinking of bed when there was a ring at the doorbell and it was the police again, needing to clear up a couple of points in my statements and review the evidence, including the letter, which they had been able to take fingerprints from, so they had to eliminate mine and anyone else's who had handled it. I could not remember who had held it and needed to think about it, and that suddenly seemed overwhelming.

I found I would peak and trough quite unexpectedly in the days after David's death. I would, at one moment, want to do everything and then, at the next, want to do nothing, as if I were conducting an experiment in mourning, testing rival approaches, keeping busy or doing nothing. I did both and the results were roughly the same, making no difference if I attempted to micromanage the catering or just go back to bed and listen to the church clock chime.

The chime would soon be ringing in the New Year, another celebration I was in no mood for, and I declined kind invitations so I could sit it out at home. My friend Beth was coming up to sit it out with me on the strict understanding that there would be no Auld Lang Syne, no mazel tov (she's Jewish), and bed by ten on New Year's Eve.

Beth arrived by train at the station. I say arrived, it was more a sort of fall, for she is as surefooted as a toddler, as short-sighted as a mole, and incredibly generous, and would not dream of arriving anywhere not bearing gifts. Laden, clumsy and unable to see, she somehow made it onto the platform and I helped her with her bags, for the weekend, of presents, of carefully sealed tubs of chicken soup with kneidlach – a favourite of both David's and mine – that she had got from Harry Morgan's in St John's Wood. We had celebrated David's fortieth birthday there, at a table of both Jews and Gentiles, for David, birthday boy, who was both Jew and Gentile, at least culturally. He is the only Gentile I have ever known to like Gefilte fish, a delicacy which for me ranks with lutefisk as the least prepossessing in world cuisine.

Chicken soup is another matter, and nourished by this most comforting of foods, Beth offered to make a start on David's affairs. David was a better starter than a finisher; a waterfall of enthusiasm would dissipate its energies quickly and leave still pools of abandonment. The next enthusiasm would come, and rather than tidy the former up to make space for the latter, David would shift location. He had a study and studio upstairs, and these had become no-go areas, crammed with the kit and relics of spent passions – a giant professional photocopier, a concert harp, an altar – and he had colonised other spaces too: the boat, the boathouse, the summer house built for me to write in, from which I was now barred, the garage which had been converted half into a barbershop, complete with walk-in sun bed, and a pottery, complete with wheel and kiln. Stuffed into whatever crack he could find were the necessary documents to make sense of his financial affairs, his pension, the boat, the cars, the dogs, and I simply could not work out how to begin getting them into order. 'Leave it to me,' said Beth, and installed me on the dining room table with a small and manageable pile of things that needed my attention, my signature, a note, while she tooled up for the job with rubber gloves and an apron and a roll of bin bags, and walked into the maelstrom of David's studio like Captain Oates into the Antarctic winter. I half expected her to say, 'I may be some time.'

This produced in me a mixture of relief – I was so glad it was not me having to do it – and apprehension, because I half feared what would turn up, and that I would discover truths about David that he had hidden from me. It had happened to someone I know, who discovered after her husband's unexpected death that he had two other households, in the unpromising locales of Watford and Chester, with dependants about whom she knew absolutely nothing, and of whom she had no intimation, and for whom she was expected to make provision out of her husband's semi-exhausted estate.

We all have our secrets, and death reveals them. Nothing could have made me love David less, he gave me quite enough to have to deal with in life and my love was unshakeable, but post-mortem administration is unsparing in the account it renders of what someone really wanted, and feared, and tried to hide. One of the first items on that balance sheet was untaken medication. I do not mean the odd strip of Zopiclone, but the serious medication that I had to pick up practically by the carrier bag from the pharmacy because David was embarrassed to do it himself. We found bottle after rattling bottle of tablets, prescribed, paid for, fetched, but not taken, and I wondered why, and what had been the effect on his health, as rickety as step ladders even when he was obeying doctor's orders. Had he surrendered? I have often heard medics talk about patients turning their heads to the wall. Crowding behind bottle after bottle of untaken tablets is the question why. Why did you not take the pills? Why did you turn your face to the wall? Why could I not stop you?

In the afternoon we drove to Pitsford Reservoir near Northampton where there's a bike shop that specialises in eBikes. I have always loved cycling, and used to be diligent and tireless, but in my fifties I had got busier and tired more easily, and fat, and I just stopped doing it. A friend in similar straits had an epiphany with eBikes and became evangelical about them and nagged me to get one, but it was vetoed by David who reminded me that I had a dozen bikes, from mountain bikes to folders to Dutch roadsters, each one a necessary upgrade to replace the last, according to me, but none of which, according to him, I used. The eBike would be my salvation, providing pedal assist so that the long unforgiving hill which leads to the end of Finedon where the church and vicarage stand would no longer defeat me, and salutary because in the past when I have had to haul myself out of a hole I have cycled. This is partly exercise, partly being in landscape, partly forward motion from your own effort. Would those benefits still accrue with electrical assistance?

Beth sat in the cafe while I test-rode a bike, which shed its chain on the first circuit, but I was already sold. I chose a Kalkhoff Agattu, lovely German model, step-through, what used to be called a women's frame, with no crossbar to impede a skirt or, indeed, cassock, and we loaded it into the back of the car and brought it home. I took it out and laboured up the hill until I worked out the best setting – eco, tour, sport or turbo, sexier names than the delivery of power deserved – but it works, giving sufficient assistance when you pedal to get you up the hill. And I knew I would need assistance to get up the hill.

New Year's Eve. In this parish it was the custom to ring it in, which produced what I think is a unique distinction. A Mr Moon was one of the ringers at the end of the reign of Queen Victoria, who died in 1901. Mr Moon died in the same year, 1901, but also in 1900. I do not know of anyone else having two dates of death, unless you include those who lived when the Julian calendar was replaced by the Gregorian. Not Mr Moon, who achieved this by ringing in the New Year as 1900 became 1901, the exertion of which caused him to have a heart attack and expire exactly on the stroke of midnight, hence the double date.

In the past, David and I used to go away for New Year, to friends in Kent, and then, when getting away got more difficult, to Althorp. This year it was just Beth and me and the dogs, and a milestone, a hard one to mark, the first year without David, and made all the harder by the sounds of fireworks, which went on too long, and frightened the dogs, especially Audrey, the most nervous among them, who went missing as the fusillades came and went and came and went, and I found her eventually in the corner of my study, trembling behind the photocopier. Poor Audrey, I fished her out and held her in my arms, and said soothing things to her. But it was not really helping, for in her fear she just wanted to make a den in as distant and as dark and as safe a place as possible. Worse was to come, and there was no way of her knowing, and I felt as desolate in that moment as I ever did.

We review the passing year with the arrival of the new, but there would be none of that today. As 2020 arrived we were binge-watching a dystopian box set and eating chicken soup with kneidlach. We wished each other long life, and I remembered another New Year, and David's deeply enjoyable habit of not knowing who famous people are. We were dining with friends, and he sat next to a young fellow who said he played the piano. 'Oh, Richard's a pianist,' David said. 'Yes, I know,' said the young fellow, 'I'm a fan.' 'Well I'm sure he'd be happy to talk to you, maybe give you some advice. You could come and hear him play.' 'That would be lovely,' he said. David said we could maybe come to hear him play, and asked if he had any gigs coming up. 'I've got one next week,' he said. 'Oh, where?' 'The Hollywood Bowl.'

It was Jamie Cullum.

He once at another dinner explained the elements of employment law to the Attorney General.

I don't know how I'm going to get through this. One day follows another and I do what I have to do but I feel like I've smoked a bale of weed and I am standing in a motorway service station dressed as a velociraptor surrounded by broken crockery and everyone's gone quiet.

New Year

New Year's Day, and a text arrived. It was from a parishioner to inform me that his brother-in-law, Matthew, had been murdered. He was in Buenos Aires with his family on a Christmas break. They had just arrived at their hotel and were suddenly attacked by *motochorros*, thieves on motorbikes, who spot rich visitors arriving at the airport and follow them to their hotels to rob them. Easy pickings, or would have been had Matthew been someone who would easily surrender his watch and wallet. The gun at first misfired, and Matthew, perhaps thinking it was not loaded, resisted, and in front of his wife and mother and stepson was shot to death. It was all over the news. His mother, Sylvia, who lives just behind the vicarage in the old gatehouse to the Hall, had just arrived home. Sylvia and her husband Jim are great benefactors to Finedon, and when I buried him the church was full. I was off work, of course, but this was not a duty I would, or would want to, hand to someone else, so I called round, in mufti, and we sat at the kitchen table and we held each other's hands, both bereaved, she of her son, me of my love, and we prayed for each other, not priest to parishioner, but fellow casualties of the war with death. It is a war we win, we both knew that, and weeping we make our alleluias over the grave, but it is a victory in which it is hard sometimes to rejoice.

Beth, who had sacrificed her New Year for mine (although she of course had the option of Rosh Hashanah, Jewish New Year), had managed to find and file piles of documents from the chaos of David's study and she presented these on the dining room table. Car, Land Rover, Morris Minor, Boat, Pension, Bank, Credit Cards – fat files, colour-coded for convenience – and I said I would make a start on them. I dropped her at the station and went home and sat at the dining room table and opened a file and took one page from it, and it was too much. My appetite for getting things done had burned out and I now felt instead a sort of dead weight, which came on like paralysis when I had to do even the most straightforward task of post-mortem tidying, so I stopped.

Friends in the parish called and asked if I fancied going to see a film. Yes, I did, *Cats*, which was getting extraordinarily bad reviews, and I was curious to see how it had gone so wrong. 'OK,' they said, and I perhaps sensed that agreement was on the grounds of sympathy rather than anticipation. They picked me up and we went to Rushden Lakes, where one of those new multiplex venues that looks like a giant shiny cube had opened. We loaded up with what must be one of the most marked-up commodities in history, cinema popcorn, and I felt self-conscious holding my tub in the lobby as people went in, as if I were neglecting the proper solemnity of my widowed state, and should be at home, in black, stroking a whimpering dog.

I don't know if it wholly deserved the terrible reviews it got, and I was not in the best of shape, but it really was not great. One of our party loved it, but he cries in Christmas adverts, one fell asleep, one thought it OK, the other like me tried to feel warmly about it but failed. I could not work out why it was so bad. It had a wish-list cast, a great writer and director, they heaped money on it, and the music is by the most successful composer of musical theatre ever. Sometimes everything looks right but put it together and it just does not work. I wondered when they realised it was a turkey, and who was the person who had said it out loud first, and how it went down?

I slept badly, my dreams disturbed by catlike figures that menaced from the edges of an urban dereliction, and then I found my way to another abandoned flat that belonged to me but that I had forgotten about, and it was infested with rats.

I try to call him when I am away. I check into a hotel room and reach for my phone to say I have arrived and to ask about his day and to enquire after the dogs, and the weight of the sudden realisation that he is not there makes me feel I am in a Philip Larkin poem, alone with remorse in a mid-priced bedroom which has not quite lost the imprint of the previous tenant.

In the morning Ozzie the postman called with another huge bag of mail. I opened two items. The first was a card of condolence, and a notification that the Eucharist had been offered in memory of David, from Archbishop Michael Curry, the Presiding Bishop of the American Episcopal Church, who preached that sermon about love at the wedding of Harry and Meghan which hoisted the eyebrows of a congregation unused to that kind of thing. How kind, I thought, to think of us, and well-spotted from the United States.

The next item I opened was a horrible card, bristling with scriptural quotations to support the sender's thesis that I would be going to hell, where David was right now being tormented by eternal fire, and it would be just dandy to have the two of us reunited there.

I try not to think too much about the senders of these

kinds of letters, because I have limited room to accommodate them and would rather allocate space to other things, but I do wonder to what extent the intensity of that hostility is driven by some sort of personal problem and how much it is simply consistent with a long-established and widely observed theological tradition. I have never, not even for a moment, felt that hell fire or even a twinge of divine disapproval would be mine as a consequence of my sexuality or my life with David. David was not so confident of that, having absorbed in childhood, in a church which was particularly clear, uncompromising, and fiery about such things, that he was bad. Consciously he had reversed that, but unconsciously, as anyone who has ever suffered as a consequence of prejudice will tell you, it is a harder and more complicated task.

I called the vet and asked if she could take a look at the dogs. I was worried about them, how they were coping with the pressures of the past fortnight. Daisy and Pongo, the long-hairs, had started scratching themselves almost obsessively. I had given them all a flea treatment but it did not seem to make a difference, and Daisy's coat was looking dull and flaky. Anna has looked after the dogs for ten years, since we first arrived at Finedon, and she has become a friend, so she said she would call round.

We sat at the kitchen table and she checked them over and said there was no evidence of fleas, but said to come in and pick up some pills to help restore the natural oils in their coats, and was there anything else?

'Yes,' I said, and tears came to my eyes and I could not say anything, but wept.

She was very kind, and took my hand, and said, 'What is it?'

I said, 'I can't look after five, Anna, on my own.'

'I know,' she said. 'What do you want to do?'

154

I had spoken to our dentist, Alex, who had a dachshund already, and would take Gus. David's brother, Mark, would take H. And Irene, his mum, who already has one of Aud's puppies, Bo, said she would take Aud. This would leave the old timers, Pongo and Daisy, whose age was in double figures and I did not think it fair on them or a future owner to disrupt their lives so much. H and Gus, the younger dogs, would be fine. Gus was only a recent arrival and H was fearless and independent. Audrey was not, she was nervous and she was mine, and the thought of her pining and not understanding why she was not with me and David was a scaleable distress, small enough to be imaginable, and big enough to fill my awareness and test my resilience, and I could not stop breaking down when I thought of her. She has always been sensitive to my moods too and in the nights after David died she would burrow down under the duvet and snuggle up close to me, so I could put my arm over her and we would both fall asleep. Planning her departure, making the arrangements, felt like a betrayal as well as a loss, and it completely undid me.

'Can you give them a health check before they go to their new homes?' I said to Anna, sobbing. 'And cut their claws?'

We sat at the kitchen table, and the dogs, who love Anna and happily surrender to whatever indignities she has to visit on them, lay comfortably in her arms as she snipped, and bits of clipped claw ricocheted round the kitchen. She read their chips, and I made a note of the numbers so Mark and Alex and Irene could reregister them in their new addresses, and I had worked out what to put in their going-away bags, collars and leads, and bowls and a toy and something that smelled of me and David. They were oblivious, I think, to their imminent eviction; sometimes they would look bewildered and helpless at changes in routine, but Daisy, who was loyal to David to the point of barely tolerating me, was not doing any of those things romantic fancy says faithful dogs do: lying in front of the bedroom door, keening for her lost master, refusing even the most delectable titbits from her other master's plate. The only thing she did, and it was heart-piercing, was keep looking behind her when I took them on a walk, looking for him, and then refusing to move, so I had to put her on the lead and pull her behind me. Perhaps this was just her, most wilful of dogs, expressing an opinion about me and the inadequacy of my command, rather than a devotion to her missing master, I don't know. We project on our dogs motives that we imagine would be our own, and I wonder if my guilt and distress at rehoming the others, and losing Aud in particular, was not something that was in sync with whatever they were feeling; but then I would dissolve miserably into tears thinking of Audrey, uncomprehending, whimpering for home, and for me.

Anna, who spends much of her professional life around people dissolving into tears because of what they think an animal is feeling, was calm and rational. 'You've made the right decision. They're going to good homes. It will be tough, but it's the right thing to do. And you will be able to see them whenever you want.' She was right, I knew she was, but loss is loss, and the lesser loss, rather a loss of dimensions I could grasp, breached my defences against the greater unimaginable loss, and when that happened I felt like I was marooned in the deserts of Louisiana like Des Grieux, mad with grief.

The headstone designs take shape. On his, David Coles, Priest 1976–2019, *on mine,* Richard Coles, Priest, 1962–20__, *two blank spaces to be filled with the digits indicating my date of death, when I will be with him again, lying under the headstones, which will speak to each other, not only by design, lettering and materials, but through Scripture. I choose a text adapted from a verse of Psalm 65 to begin on his and end on mine, although each could stand alone. On his it reads:*

'Thy clouds drop fatness, they shall drop upon the dwellings of the wilderness, and the little hills shall rejoice on every side.'

On mine, the response:

'The folds shall be full of sheep, the valleys also shall stand so thick with corn, that they shall laugh and sing.'

The Sentences

I was dreading the funeral. I normally like them, and pride myself on doing a good one, but this was David's funeral, and I was principal mourner, not officiant, and – highly unusual for me – I was not sure how I would feel about being on parade in front of so many. But it had to be done.

David's family had driven down from Lancashire the day before and checked in to a hotel. We met at my church at five on the eve of his funeral, them in funeral clothes, me in choir dress, cassock and cotta and purple stole. It was almost darkest night, and I showed them to a pew at the front and then went to meet Jonathan, the funeral director, and the bearers, who had arrived with the waiting hearse at the lych gate. Seeing the love of your life boxed for burial is a moment in which the world stops, but I was on duty, and there was a liturgy that needed an officiant. I led the cortège into church saying the Sentences, short texts from the Authorised Version, which are so familiar and so apt, I know them by heart.

They begin with '"I am the resurrection and the life," says the Lord . . .' It is the first thing the congregation at a funeral hears, and because it is so familiar it has a similar effect to the Wedding March from *Lohengrin*; it makes people who are sitting stand up.

'Those who believe in me, even though they die, will live,

and everyone who lives and believes in me will never die.' We moved slowly up the aisle and I thought of the countless times David and I had walked up this aisle in our ten years at Finedon.

'I am convinced that neither death, nor life, nor angels, nor rulers, nor things present, nor things to come, nor powers, nor height, nor depth, nor anything else in all creation, will be able to separate us from the love of God in Christ Jesus our Lord.' We had together taken weddings and funerals, Evensongs and Eucharists, preached sermons, swung thuribles, sung hymns.

'Since we believe that Jesus died and rose again, even so, through Jesus, God will bring with him those who have died. So we will be with the Lord for ever. Therefore encourage one another with these words.' I recalled when one of our parishioners was chairman of the county council we had the annual service of thanksgiving in our church, and the lord lieutenant, and the chain gangs from all the towns of the county, and the great and the good were gathered, and it all went very well until the procession out when I sensed something was wrong and as we left through the south door I looked behind me and saw that David, vested in choir dress, had fallen asleep, and as the chancel emptied of dignitaries was revealed, lightly snoring, to the entire congregation.

'We brought nothing into the world, and we take nothing out. The Lord gave, and the Lord has taken away; blessed be the name of the Lord.' It also occurred to me that the only thing lacking from our trips up this aisle or any aisle was our marriage, not an option in church, for the law did not permit it, nor for us in the civil jurisdiction, for the bishop could not issue us with a licence if that were to happen. David had always wanted to get married, to upgrade, as he put it, when the law was changed to allow for this. I was not so bothered, content with a civil partnership if it meant being acceptable to the authorities. I did not want to turn the formal recognition of our relationship into an issue. One of the most difficult things for clergy in intimate relationships is to preserve a necessary private realm for those relationships, and it is difficult because the Church tends to take hold of everything, and turn it into a sermon, or a test of orthodoxy, or simply make the private public. I also didn't want to lose my licence and, as a result, my parish. So we had reached a compromise. When I retired, we would get married, first thing, and have a big do, and deal with the more manageable consequences then.

'The steadfast love of the Lord never ceases, his mercies never come to an end; they are new every morning; great is his faithfulness.' But we skipped the wedding, and went straight to the funeral, and our last walk together up the aisle, or rather my walk, and his trundle, was for a parting not a union.

'Blessed are those who mourn, for they will be comforted.'

The coffin was placed on the coffin stand in front of the chancel arch, where the Creation meets the Creator, wrong way round, priest style, with the head at the feet and the feet at the head, and together with his family I dressed it in the customary way. The funeral pall, in midnight blue and purple, is laid over, like a king-size bedspread on a child's single bed, and a Bible and crucifix are laid on top of that, and four large candles on stands are lit.

I started to read the service but my voice gave way for a moment, and I saw Jonathan the funeral director look up from the back to see if I would be all right. That put me back on track, and I made it to the end.

I locked the church, with David in it, and got changed and we went for supper at a pub down the road. His clan had turned out in force, from his Uncle Alan, who is a thrilling tenor and would perform 'I Walk with God' as we left church the following day, to his youngest nephew Ned, who had lasted as long as he could in this adult discourse of loss and memory, and found distraction in his Gameboy between main course and sweet. It felt like a lapse of manners that David was on his own in church, when he should be with us, and I understood the Irish Catholic custom of inviting the deceased, in an open coffin, to the party celebrating the extinguished life; but I liked hearing his family exchanging stories of David as a son and brother, a nephew and uncle, for I was discovering life in him that I had not discovered before and it was an act of resistance to death, whose spoils were the life of the him I knew.

Later I went back to church and took Daisy, because I wanted to give her, his most faithful friend, the opportunity to say goodbye to him, and to see if there would be any sign of doggy faithfulness, like Greyfriars Bobby, who lay on his master's grave in Edinburgh so impressively they put up a statue of him after he too had gone to his reward. I had read that the whole story was a fiction, and Daisy did nothing to restore confidence in its veracity. She showed no sign at all of grief, or even recognition, and ignored his mortal remains entirely, apart from burrowing her way curiously under the pall on her customary patrol of the olfactory indicators of small mammals.

I sat in my stall in the chancel, the last time David and I would be alone together until I too am buried. I said the Office for the Dead from my prayer book. I liked the sound of it, not just the cadences of the psalms that I know so well, with their reminder that what we are doing has been done before and will be done again, but because it is an Office, the word in this context meaning part of the daily routine of prayer, which makes it sound businesslike and tidy.

When I had finished, Daisy uncurled from around my feet, and we left. At the west end of the church I switched out the lights and looked back to see David's coffin, dressed in blue and purple, and lit by the dim and flickering light of candles, and the floodlights, which illuminate the church by night, and half fire up the stained glass so that the saints and angels and cherubim appear more tentatively than usual in the great East Window. His coffin looked like it was moving away, a trick of the angle and the light, and I wished, like Orpheus, I had not looked back.

The night before his funeral he came to me in a dream.

He just walked in through the front door and I was surprised and said, 'But I thought you were dead?' And he said, 'No, I just wanted a break,' and I realised that he had gone on holiday, decided unilaterally, which seemed a bit peculiar, but it was nice to see him and I was pleased he was not dead. Then he said, 'But I've met someone else so I'm only here to pick up my stuff,' but all the stuff he wanted I had thrown away and he was angry with me, and Audrey ran away, and the dream ended with me alone on a howling, dark and rainy night driving down dripping lanes in the Land Rover, looking for her.

It woke me up. It was five in the morning, and the dogs, all five, were curled up with me on, and in, the bed. I checked to see that Audrey, lost in my dream, was safe, and she was, lodged firmly into my belly. But it was for the last time and so I lay for a while and hugged them all close, except for Daisy, not given to such needy display, and in the end it was her peremptory bark to be let out that ended the tableau.

I fed them, and myself, and got up, and took them out for a walk as dawn broke, all five, hoping that there would be no one else around at that hour. I thought for a second how ironic it would be if one ran off and disappeared on the day they were to be dispatched to their new homes.

I got changed into clericals, black suit, and went over to church to meet Jonathan. We took the cross and Bible and pall off the coffin and wheeled him on the trolley from place of honour to the old choir vestry, where he lay surrounded by flower pedestals and superannuated hymn books, even in death having to cede his place to the needs of the parish; how he would have disliked that.

I walked back to the vicarage just as two friends of mine from Glasgow parked on Church Hill, so they came in and we had a couple of minutes to talk before Jonathan arrived to pick me up, and we drove in the funeral limousine to the hotel at Kettering for one o'clock to meet David's family.

David's father and brothers and his older nephews were going to bear the coffin, so Jonathan gave them a run-through of what that important duty entails, foremost of which is not dropping the coffin, which is much heavier than people imagine. Funeral professionals always notice that in films coffins are invariably empty and handle much more easily than they do when full. Also, the head is the heaviest part, so when the coffin is hoisted to shoulder height there is an extra pair of hands at that end to provide the necessary lift to keep it even. I remember once seeing a production of the Ring Cycle and Siegfried's dead body was hoisted without this provision during the Death March and the poor tenor's head was jerked so severely I thought he might not be acting.

There was no small talk in the funeral limousine, not even between me and Jonathan sitting up front and separated from the others by a discreet divider. We were overtaken by an ambulance with blue lights flashing and siren blaring. Normally when this happens gallows funeral humour dictates that someone will say 'they're playing our tune', but no one did, even if they thought it, as I did.

I was half dreading, half hoping, that when we got to Finedon it would be full of people unable to find somewhere to park, arriving late and cross, but there were places enough in the streets, and in the church. We pulled in at the lych gate where my brothers and their families were waiting, Andy in a new and improbable hat, a black Homburg. An unexpected face too, of a colleague at the BBC, and I had a moment of cognitive dissonance, wondering how he was connected to my nieces, until I realised he had simply arrived at the same time as us.

The tenor bell was tolling, weak winter light was filtering through the trees, and a crew from ITV News, at a discreet distance, filmed us walking up the path towards the south door. I wondered if they would be disappointed that there was no coffin, already in place in the church, and if they would wait for the end to get us going out, or if they had to go to Wisbech to film the mayor switching on a biomass boiler instead. I went through the porch into church, through which I had passed with dozens of bereaved families, but this was my family and I was principal mourner and I felt something I have so rarely felt before – at all, in adulthood – and I did not at first understand what it was. Jonathan the organist was playing Vaughan Williams' 'Rhosymedre', as requested, and I had to look ahead as we made our way up the aisle to the front pews, towards Martyn, the officiant, towards the choir in their stalls, and towards David's coffin restored to its place in front of the chancel arch. The only face I remember seeing was that of my best friend, Matthew, who had come up from Devon with his wife Di. I remembered looking at him at their wedding at Widdecombe a quarter of a century earlier, and seeing on his finger the fresh band of gold, bright and striking, because it changed everything. Here we are, I thought, entering the zone when it is funerals, not weddings or baptisms, that change everything and are the milestones from now on.

Martyn greeted us, we sang 'Dear Lord and Father of Mankind', and Mark gave the address, off the cuff, funny, generous and truthful, and it must have had some surprises for those who only knew David through me to hear of his working-class background, his upbringing in a fundamentalist church, his first marriage. Mark had asked me at the hotel earlier if there was anything I wanted him to say, and he had typed it into his phone. He read it out:

'I loved him, and he loved me, I am so grateful for the time we had together. And if anyone knows where the keys to the Land Rover are, could they please let me know.'

As the choir sang Psalm 121 to the chant by Walford Davies, I looked at the Order of Service, left for me in the pew. I had chosen two photographs of David, one on the front of him looking happy holding H, taken when we were on holiday in Yorkshire, and on the back one of him paddle-boarding in Kintyre, a tiny figure way out at sea with Ailsa Craig faintly visible in the background. Hello, I'm here, and goodbye, I'm floating away.

The Lord himself is thy keeper: the Lord is thy defence upon thy right hand;
So that the sun shall not burn thee by day: neither the moon by night.

Lucy read the passage from Ephesians – *Although I am the very least of all the saints, this grace was given to me to bring to the Gentiles the news of the boundless riches of Christ* – and Jonathan sang 'Climb Ev'ry Mountain'.

Kate read the story of the Princess and the Pea – *They could see she was a real princess and no question about it, now that she had felt one pea all the way through twenty mattresses and twenty more feather beds. Nobody but a princess could be so sensitive. So the prince made haste to marry her, because he knew he had found a real princess* – and we sang 'How Shall I Sing That Majesty?', which David loved, but I had printed the words the wrong way round in the Order of Service and the choir sang something different from the rest of us. I winced and thought how I would be marked down by the clergy in the congregation, and marked down too for not having a Requiem Mass, or by others for not having the coffin carried in, or the right kind of flowers. Imagined criticisms buzzed round me like mosquitoes as Martyn gave the address. All clergy do this, I think, when our services are attended by other clergy, even this service, and professional matters were just more available to me in that moment than a grief too great to feel and to express.

We prayed for David, the congregation prayed for us, and then I performed my only liturgical role in the service.

As the choir and congregation stood to sing 'Guide Me O Thou Great Redeemer' I approached the coffin and took from a side table one of David's favourite pots by one of his favourite potters, Lisa Hammond. It contained Holy Water from a bottle that he had filled from the river Jordan when we took the parish there on pilgrimage. I took also a branch of rosemary from the bush he had planted in the vicarage garden, and I dipped it into the water and walked slowly round the coffin, sprinkling it as I went. It's an ancient custom, the asperges, washing away our sin, a reminder of our baptism, the fulfilment of its promise, and a way through the waters of death into new life.

When I tread the verge of Jordan
Bid my anxious fears subside;
Death of death, and hell's destruction,
Land me safe on Canaan's side:
Songs and praises, songs and praises,
I will ever give to thee,
I will ever give to thee.

Vinnie and Mark and Andrew and Jamie and Charlie and Joey and Terry, David's father and brothers and nephews and best friend, shouldered the coffin and led us out. I walked behind with Irene, holding her hand, and I could not really bear to look left and right, but saw some people I knew, one of my former producers from the BBC, three clergy in a row – David's training incumbent from Wymondham, and two contemporaries of mine from theological college – my editor and colleagues from *Saturday Live*, someone I was at school with, my cousin; and they looked at me with the tentative 'how are you?' expression that those who love you adopt when you are on parade in this most exposing and exacting way. There I understood what I was feeling, something so unusual for me I did not at first recognise it: I did not want to be the centre of attention.

I was glad to be out. We stowed David in the hearse, and then family and close friends, and Jane, my curate, drove to Grafton Underwood, where we had always planned to end our days, and where half of that compact was about to be fulfilled. We stopped at the little bridge over the village brook and regrouped at the bottom of the path that leads up to the churchyard. The light was just beginning to fade, and there was a faint pearly mist which shone in the slanted light. Good weather for a burial.

I turned round and saw to one side the men with the

digger who had dug the grave, and were waiting discreetly to fill it in, and to the other the union flag flying at half-mast from the Manor House, home of the lord lieutenant, whom I had last seen in A&E when David was admitted for the last time.

The pallbearers led us slowly up to the north side of the church, past the chancel where former vicars of the parish were buried, the Hon'bles and the canons, second and third and fourth sons and cousins of the Dukes of Buccleuch, on whose estate the village stands, to where David's grave await-ed. The coffin was lowered in as Jane said the words that I have said dozens and dozens of times, when I have buried partners, and daughters, and grandparents, and cousins, and the great, and the wicked, and those whom no one would ever mourn, and those whom no one even noticed, differen-tiated according to gender, not status.

We have entrusted our brother David to God's mercy,
and we now commit his body to the ground:
earth to earth, ashes to ashes, dust to dust:
in sure and certain hope of the resurrection to eternal life
through our Lord Jesus Christ,
who will transform our frail bodies
that they may be conformed to his glorious body,
who died, was buried, and rose again for us.
To him be glory for ever.
Amen.

I remember wondering how long it would be before I pronounced my first non-gendered committal, and then I stepped forward and took a handful of earth from the box, helpfully extended towards me, and dropped it into the grave. It rattled on the coffin. I followed it with a yellow rose that Irene gave me. It gently thudded onto the coffin. Then everyone formed a solemn queue and did the same. We stood in silence, save the sound of weeping.

The poignancy of this moment was mitigated by an urgent need to pee – when this happens to you, remember to take every opportunity to use the lavatory. My sister-in-law Julia, who lives in the village, had arranged for the church to be open, so I invoked principal mourner privilege and was first in. Another, less solemn, queue formed outside.

The church of St James at Grafton Underwood is a lovely twelfth-century building, little and crooked, and dignified with sculptures which seem too grand for it, commemorating various members of the Montague, Douglas and Scott families, conjoined in the Dukedom of Buccleuch. The south aisle has the only depiction in stained glass of a Flying Fortress, commemorating the United States Air Force which was based here in the Second World War on a huge abandoned airfield where, in childhood, my mother used to let us drive her car round and round.

The lovely winter evening light illuminated the new windows that had just been installed by Tom Denny, a gift of the lord lieutenant, lovely things on the theme of Genesis, in tawny Evensong colours, one of them showing the brook and the church and standing in front of them a figure embracing another figure, like a father and a son, a prodigal perhaps, and that made my heart contract, and I prayed for David in the loving and forgiving embrace of his creator, beyond suffering and sadness.

We drove back to Finedon, where refreshments were being served at the cricket club. By the time we arrived many at the funeral had left, but even though the crowd had thinned there were unmanageably high numbers of people to see and the hour or so I spent there is a blur. I talked to Matthew, who had waited, and he hugged me and said he had to go, but to come down to Devon where we could spend some proper time together. Simon, my old producer, embraced me too. I sat with an interesting overlap of two worlds, my friend Beth and her sister and another friend from my lunch club who knew them in the complex network of north London's Jewish geography. I talked a bit to my Scottish friends, who had come down from Glasgow and from Edinburgh, who have turned out for so many occasions in my life, and I for theirs, weddings and baptisms, and now a funeral. They overlap with Lorna, who had volunteered to stay with me for a couple of days, and to continue the brave and good work of Beth, sorting out the chaos of David's affairs.

As soon as I could I said, 'Can we go?' and Lorna and the Scottish friends walked back with me as the darkness fell and the spire of the church began to glow orange as the flood-lights came on. Almost as soon as I was in, the doorbell rang. It was Alex, our dentist, and her husband Duncan, who were taking General Guster, the most recent of our dogs to arrive. I handed him over to his new owners, with his going-away bag, and as they left I had to dive into my study, unable to contain the sorrow which overwhelmed me. I tried to gulp down some air but got grief-hiccups and then felt breathless.

The doorbell rang again. It was Mark, David's brother, who was taking H. I remembered the day he arrived. David asked me to come into the kitchen and open a lidded basket on the kitchen table, and there he was, tiny and blinking. He was still tiny and blinking, equally bemused by everything, as Mark carried him away. 'I won't hang around,' he said, 'Cas and the boys are in the car . . .'

Another ring on the doorbell. It was Irene and Vinnie, who were taking Audrey. I have always felt a helpless attachment to Aud, partly because of her nervousness and the way she would cling to me when she wasn't full of beans and curiosity and venturing into the world. I remember when she arrived, it was just before Mayday, which we celebrate on the lawn of the old vicarage by maypole dancing, performing a mummers' play, and crowning the May Queen. I took Audrey to show to the kids and she was so frightened she peed all down my cassock. She turned out in the long run to have both strength and steadiness, the mother to six puppies, fathered by H, the first litter before he was one, so tiny, so potent. David, far broodier than me, had encouraged a rematch and a second litter arrived, including Bo, who went to Vinnie and Irene, and was waiting at home for the arrival of her mother – not that dogs, in my experience, are sentimental about such things.

Just then, as I was handing her over, another ring on the doorbell, and it was a police officer who needed to see me about the investigation into the hostile letters and emails. By the time I had him settled in my study, Audrey was gone, so I did not have to see her wriggling to escape between the front door and the car, or looking through the back window at the retreating vicarage, or whimpering all the way up the M6, as I knew she would.

It had to be done. There could be no better home for her. But I still cannot think of her without feeling grief come rumbling in, like thunder, or the tide.

Everyone went except Lorna. I was so glad it was her, because with her I do not have to try, or dissemble, or entertain, or be 'insightful'. The funeral had been an ordeal. I had not expected to be moved by it because, like the host of too many parties, after a while in making them work for others they cease to work for you, and the softening effects of liturgy and solemnity and doing things properly no longer have their palliative effect. I thought of his coffin in the earth, not with the handful of dust I had thrown in rattling on the lid, but with three tons of earth unceremoniously dropped on it when the diggers filled it in. He was now six feet under, decomposing, a far more vivid image for me than someone floating through the air towards a dazzling light.

And now, with the funeral behind me, I had no excuse to delay turning to the files of papers that Beth had put together, all of which needed my attention, and then there were his things, his clothes, and letters, and embroidery, and toiletries, and all the things so meaningful for him that he could not part with them, but now he was dead they lost meaning, many of them, and became ballast, junk, rubbish, because nothing of him adhered in them that I could shore up against his loss.

That night, after everyone was gone except Lorna, I picked up a takeaway, and we ate it in our scampers in front of the fire and talked.

'Are you OK?' she asked.

No, and from deep within grief flowed up like lava. My tears were hot and rolled down my cheeks and my throat was tight, and breathing came in gasps. I was trying, as always, to speak in sentences, and started quoting something I had posted on Facebook, something I thought rather fine and sensitive, but what I was trying to say, how I was trying to rationalise what was happening to me was not enough, nowhere near, and what I needed to do was howl, and Lorna just let me do it, saying nothing, not flinching, waiting until the gale had blown itself out.

This is what I wanted. I wanted old, close friends to be strong and steady and present. I did not want to be left alone to grieve, I did not want to pretend that I was all right, I did not want people to look away nervously if I began to cry. Not everyone can do this, for all sorts of reasons, and if you can be forgiving, forgive it, because deaths and bereavement are difficult to handle and not everyone does it well. I did find that I remembered who delivered, and who did not, and while I have not trimmed the Christmas card list as a result, I have, without conscious decision, resolved to spend what limited resources of time and attention I have on people who wish to return them in roughly the same proportion. Bereavement has for me accelerated a process that was already happening, that must happen, I think, as we get older. People who were originally listed as friends migrate to the acquaintance list. The broad friendships of our youth become unsustainable, we don't have the time, or the shared experience, or the inclination. Also, if I am going to rely on someone, and have them rely on me, there are great advantages if they know me, have seen the best of me, and the worst of me, and are still standing. As I get older I don't want people to see the worst of me. It would be like the unthinkable horror of having to share a bathroom.

The bed's too big without you, I thought, now there were only three of us instead of the usual seven, David and three dachshunds having vacated the north side of our super-king-size, upgraded over the years to accommodate our menagerie and his restless leg syndrome. I still sleep on the south side, and the dogs too, as if migrating to fill available space would still be a trespass. I still expect him to come back, and to want his place restored, and his things recovered.

The next day Lorna appeared in a pinny. 'What's to go, and what's to stay?' We worked out three categories – stay, go, awaiting decision – and she disappeared into David's study and studio, and I mean disappeared because beyond the open door lay what looked like an obstacle course from

Jeux sans frontières, and it exercised her, slight and nimble though she is, to squeeze a way through.

All through the morning I sat at the dining room table opening correspondence, and putting it into piles, while Lorna went up and down the stairs, carrying bag after black plastic bag. The dogs eventually settled at my feet until I took them out for a walk, and I came across one of my Romanian parishioners, who gave me his condolences, and told me he sympathised especially because when he was a boy of eight he lost his father, who died of a stroke aged only thirty-nine in the hard winter of 1969 when snow had fallen snow on snow and was so thick he couldn't be buried in their grave-yard but had to be taken to higher ground outside Bucharest. 'It's terrible, isn't it?' he said. 'Yes,' I said, 'it is. How did you cope?' 'We have a saying in Romania, "Death is death, but food is food."' I took this to mean the necessities of living come before any other consideration and so I went home and started making a cauliflower cheese.

Lorna and I ate it as she went through the list of what she had uncovered, discovered, recovered, and after half a dozen or so items I was losing the will to live, and must have faded, in spite of maintaining, I thought, my interested face, a necessary technique for vicaring. She has known me long enough not to be taken in by such things, so she stopped and said, 'Rich, what are you going to do?'

'I don't know. They say not to make any plans for a while.'

'I don't mean next month or next year, I mean in the long term?'

'I don't know.'

'Why don't you come and live with me?'

This was no casual offer. Lorna and I had been flatmates, off and on, for nearly forty years. We had always said when we were young that we would see each other out, and indulged a fantasy of pottering around English cathedral cities in old age, like characters from a Barbara Pym novel. Life happened, for both of us circumstances changed, but now, four decades later, that fond wish was a possibility. Neither of us had immediate dependants, we were solvent, and had a reasonable expectation of remaining so, had no asymmetrical needs, and complementary if not identical pleasures.

'That would be great.'

On the last lovely weekend of autumn, Vinnie and Irene come to stay. Because of lockdown it is the first time we have seen each other since David died. They bring Audrey, who runs through the opened vicarage door like Usain Bolt and throws herself at Daisy and Pongo, and then at me, squeaking with excitement.

Irene has brought parkin, a gift each autumn, and we sit in the garden as the dogs play, and over tea and cake we talk about David, as the garden he planted gives its last flourish before the cold weather, a flourish of dahlias, and zinnias, and the last of the roses, which have come and come and come since June.

We go to visit David's grave, and leave the yellow roses he loved there, and we talk about how we are doing. I can only really talk about this as I want to, need to, to his parents, whose loss is different, but as keen; and we weep.

Later we take the dogs for a walk through the fields that lie between Finedon and Great Harrowden, where David and I went nearly every day until he became ill. It is at its loveliest at this time of year, the leaves beginning to fall from the woods that border the field, lying like confetti on a church path, and the fields, ploughed and harrowed, as neat as brown corduroy.

I see a crab apple tree in a hedgerow so heavy with fruit it is begging to be picked, and after I have seen off Vinnie and Irene I return at dusk with a basket. The tree is surrounded by briars, some so lethal I pick my way between them like a Tommy through barbed wire. The fruit comes away easily; sometimes if the stalk resists before it breaks, the branch shivers, and the apples drop straight into my basket.

At home I wash them, trim them, cut the larger ones in half; they give a bittersweet odour. I boil them in the preserving pan my grandmother gave my mother, and my mother gave me, until they're soft enough to mash into a pulp. I pour the pulp into a jelly bag rigged up on a stand in the utility room and set over a two-litre jug. The juice begins to drip through. Before I go to bed I let the dogs out and find the jug half full of a green pearly luscious liquid, with the hint of blush, I think.

I am going to make crab apple jelly; bittersweet preserve.

In the morning the jug is almost full, more juice than I thought the pulp would produce, and I need to find some more jam jars. I know we have some somewhere. I find them, eventually, in the garage on a shelf, and beneath them are a dozen jars filled with a dark garnet-coloured filling.

Vicarage Plum Jam 2019, *say the labels, in David's wobbly sickroom writing. I take a jar to the kitchen and am about to spread some on buttered toast when I think, How much of him is left? Do I want to eat this or keep it? Should I enjoy it like the gift he intended it to be? Or should I hang on to it like Miss Havisham her wedding breakfast?*

I cannot decide, so I put it back.

While I sterilise the empty jars I have found in the oven, I boil the crab apple juice with an amount of sugar that seems dangerously excessive, skimming off a horrible gluey scum which makes me doubt the desired clarity and colour of the end product will materialise.

I pour, and seal, and leave to cool.

In the evening I return and take one of the jars outside into the garden. It is still sunny, and when I hold up the jar it glows, ruby-gold, and the light seems almost to dance in it.

Acknowledgements

I would like to thank my agent, Tim Bates, and all at PFD; my publisher, Alan Samson, and all at Weidenfeld & Nicolson; my PA, R.J. Baxter; and my parishioners.